Self-Expansion
Through
Marriage

Self-Expansion

Through

Marriage

A Way to Inner Happiness

Swami Kriyananda

Crystal Clarity Publishers
Nevada City, California

Crystal Clarity Publishers, Nevada City, CA 95959
Copyright © 1995 Hansa Trust
All rights reserved. Published 2012

Printed in China.
Third Edition
ISBN13: 978-1-56589-268-2
eISBN: 978-1-56589-512-6

Cover design, interior design and layout by Tejindra Scott Tully

Library of Congress Cataloging-in-Publication Data

Kriyananda, Swami.
    Self-expansion through marriage : a way to inner happiness /
        Swami Kriyananda. -- 3rd ed.
        p. cm.
    Previous edition published under title: Expansive Marriage :
        A Way to Self-Realization, 1995.
        ISBN 978-1-56589-268-2 (pbk. : alk. paper) --
        ISBN 978-1-56589-512-6 (epub)
    1. Marriage. 2. Self-realization. I. Title.

HQ734.W197 2012
204'.41--dc23

www.crystalclarity.com **/** 800.424.1055 – 530.478.7600

Contents

Foreword

by Susan M. Campbell, Ph.D.,
author of *The Couple's Journey, Beyond the Power Struggle,*
and *Survival Strategies for the New Workplace*

In these times of cultural upheaval, the institution of marriage, like so many social norms, faces profound challenges. Marriages based on "feeling good" and "meeting each other's needs" have proved disappointing. New insights are needed, based on universal truths but capable, at the same time, of adaptation to changing circumstances.

We live in a world, and even more so in an era, in which, as the ancient maxim puts it, "all is flux." The greater the flux, or outward change, the greater the need in our lives for something stable, a spiritual center within ourselves to which to relate our ever-changing experiences. In marriage, what our culture needs today is a new paradigm for relationships, one that embraces both the outward institution and an inner process of self-unfoldment.

The vision implied by the title of this book, *Expansive Marriage,** speaks to both needs. "Marriage" carries the connotation of something intended, at least, to be enduring and stable. "Expansive" expresses the need to respond creatively to the *inner* challenges of marriage. In embarking on an "expansive marriage," you commit yourself to something that you know *must* change, constantly, and you welcome this fact

* The title of an earlier edition of this book.

as an opportunity for mutual as well as for self-development, looking at change itself for what it mirrors to you about your own nature. This is the essence of the new paradigm marriage: its responsiveness to change, its respect for other sides of an issue, and its increasing centeredness in a spiritual reality that never changes.

In my view, an expansive reaction to change grows out of respect for differences of opinion and outlook. Acceptance of these differences fosters a wider, more expansive resolution of the issues concerned.

I heartily agree with author J. Donald Walters's* emphasis on creativity in marriage. In my book, *The Couple's Journey*, I called it co-creativity—Stage Five on the "path toward wholeness." The earlier stages are for healing the past. The more mature stages are for shared creativity in a couple's relationship with the larger world. Co-creativity involves the man and woman in cooperative evolutionary activity leading the couple ever closer to God.

I very much appreciate also Walters's vision of marriage as a means of bringing out the best in each partner. In the past, most marriages have been comfort-oriented, not expansion-oriented. But in these times of planetary crisis and change, it is time couples rose to meet the new challenges. Partners need to aspire in themselves, and to inspire one another, to live at their highest potential. Inspiration is the only way to effect meaningful change, whether in your partner or in yourself. It is time people realized that change cannot be effected through guilt and self-accusation on the one hand, or through manipulation or control on the other. Inspiration is the agent for change of the new paradigm.

* Swami Kriyananda's Western name.

Walters has obviously made the study of the human energy system a major part of his life's work. Our present culture desperately needs a more enlightened view of human energy—how to generate it, how to nurture and sustain it, and how to use it to help others and oneself. The newly emerging relationship paradigm involves a deepening understanding of *energy* in ever-subtler aspects. The vision of *expansive marriage*, with its emphasis on inspiration, creativity, and shared communion even in the practice of silence together, contributes significantly to this new paradigm by portraying a very sophisticated understanding of the concept of energy. Energy is a spiritual phenomenon. Embarking on an expansive marriage will change your relationship to the life force, pulsing through all of us, that we call "energy." As you continue further along the path of expansive marriage, you come to recognize that what you have been accustomed to think of as your personal energy is actually part of a vast ocean of energy. Expanding into this universal energy is, ultimately, what expansive marriage is all about.

It is my hope that more and more of us will make new discoveries on this path to self-realization, that we may heal ourselves, our families, our communities, and our planet.

Susan M. Campbell
Belvedere, CA

Introduction

The reader, when presented with a book on marriage, will probably want to know the author's credentials. Is he a marriage counselor? Has he a Master's degree, or a Ph.D., to show specialization in the subject? What other books has he written on the subject?

I have spent many years counseling people—forty-five years, so far. I have worked with people all my life, both publicly and in private. I have lived in many countries, and familiarized myself with many customs and cultural attitudes, East and West. I have written some sixty books* many of them on topics directly or indirectly related to marriage. I have founded and am the spiritual leader of a large and thriving community called Ananda Village, near Nevada City, California, and of several branch communities in America and elsewhere.

My most important "credential" by far is that I studied with one of the truly wise people of this century, Paramhansa Yogananda. In a life of travels I have met many of the great and famous. None of them had the impact on me that Yogananda had. I was fortunate to study with him the last three and a half years of his life. If this book contains any wisdom, and if it proves helpful to you, it is to Yogananda's wise counseling above all that the credit is due.

One facet of his teaching was that he never imposed on others a system of beliefs. His central teaching was spiritual,

* Editor's note: By 2012, Swami Kriyananda had written more than 140 books.

yet he met people where *they* were, psychologically. Far from trying to convert them, spiritually, he helped them according to their own perceived interests and needs, offering them more if they wanted it, but not if they didn't. By his attunement with people in all walks of life and in every stage of mental maturity, he was able to help them in ways that were supremely practical.

I don't say that the ideas in this book were his. Some of them were. Some may not have been. What he gave me was an *approach*, not a system of set formulae. As he used to say, rather than give a person money, it is better to teach him how to earn money himself.

Expansive  Marriage

Chapter  One

A Direction, Not an Ending

"They married, and lived happily ever after." Isn't that how most fairy tales end? But then, that's all they are: fairy tales.

Romantic comedies, too, although they don't always say it in so many words, usually end with the same beamish promise: unalloyed wedded bliss, descending perpetually, like showers of rose petals, upon couples who, once they have tied the knot, stroll carefree through life down lushly green mossy glades.

People are conditioned from early childhood to look upon marriage as Nature's solution to the search for happiness. The handsome prince marries the beautiful princess—she of the long, golden tresses. The poor shepherd boy wins the aloof and unapproachable princess. Cinderella, after years of menial labor and of withering contempt from those closest to her, is selected from among the fairest maidens of the land to marry the noble prince.

Such a view of marriage is two-dimensional. It suggests no road disappearing gradually into the distant future, and therefore no future challenges. The couples in this picture do not walk down life's road together: They merely step into the canvas and disappear. How often has marriage, entered upon with such blithe expectations, proved disappointing!

It is natural to romanticize weddings. Brides want to wear white, and would feel deprived of something precious, if not driven to open rebellion, were it Fashion's decree that they wear tweeds. Guests want a wedding feast, and would feel cheated if all they got in return for their gifts were tortilla chips and a spiced yogurt dip. The parents want the congratulations (and perhaps the envy?) of their friends. The children want a chance to run amuck among the adults without fear of a scolding. Everybody likes a good time. And the groom— well, yes, the groom: He'll probably be happy enough, once he can get out of that stiff costume—better suited to an operetta, he thinks—and into something comfortable.

It is perfectly normal that weddings be romanticized. Marriage, however, is another story. It should be viewed realistically.

For marriage is a human state; it can give people no more than they themselves bring to it. The function of marriage is not to lift people "up to the stars." Marriage is not a substitute for divine ecstasy. All it can give people is a new recognition of what they are already, in themselves.

Given the unregenerate condition of most human beings, the self-recognition marriage bestows is not always easy to bear.

❦ An Opportunity for Growth ❦

Marriage should not be approached as a beautiful, but motionless, painting. Rather, it should be viewed as an opportunity for ever-further growth and development. It should be recognized as a challenge and an opportunity to make someone else happy, rather than pursue selfishly throughout life one's own happiness. Marriage should be undertaken creatively, as an art. Couples should seek fresh ways every day to express their love for one another, and to bring out the best in each other, and in themselves.

"Creativity" is a key word. For marriage is not, in itself, a solution. It simply provides new opportunities for finding solutions to life's problems. We may say, also, that for every solution marriage provides it also presents fresh problems to be faced, multiplied by two, and then three or more as the "blessed events" begin piling up.

Any couple who think to live "happily ever after" once the wedding bells have stopped ringing are destined for a rude awakening. Hardly will the ringing have ceased than other, strident sounds intrude themselves: the bustling traffic of other people's priorities; the dreary exigencies of bills; life's daily routine; the growing realization that marriage alone has provided no perfect fusion of two human beings, as diverse expectations manifest themselves, along with diverse tendencies for meeting those expectations.

❧ A Deeper Fulfillment ☙

The mere fact that marriage is not really likely to fulfill the roseate dreams of many romanticists doesn't mean it cannot offer deep fulfillment—deeper and more valid fulfillment, indeed, than the common two-dimensional expectations of it. What people entering marriage must do is stop dreaming and face their joint adventure not only hand in hand, but open-eyed.

Life's true fulfillments are never static. Truth itself is not static. Any definition of reality, including the highest truth, should be an attempt to point a direction. Even the greatest human fulfillment can provide only a hint of Ultimate Perfection.

It is a weakness of human nature to want to define things absolutely. Definitions serve a purpose to the extent that they stretch the mind. But they are limiting if, after stretching the mind, they impede further growth.

Years ago I gave a series of lectures in Kuranda, Queensland, in northeast Australia. At the end of the series a man came up to me and said, "I didn't attend all your lectures, but I happened to catch the end of this last one. I'm not familiar with your philosophy, but I noticed that you kept on referring to God. Well, I'm an atheist. What can you say about God that will be relevant to me?"

After a moment's thought I made a suggestion: "Why not think of God as the highest potential you can imagine for yourself?"

He paused in astonishment, then nodded in that tentative, eyebrow-raised sort of way that Australians affect to indicate a combination of wonder and approval. "I can live with that," he concluded.

Perfection in marriage, as in everything else in life, should be seen, not as a still photograph, and not as a plateau, but as continuous movement in a forever unfolding direction—movement accompanied sometimes by struggle, but movement also holding a promise of great heights to be attained.

❀ Points to Remember ❀

1. Marriage can give no more to people than they themselves bring to it.

2. Marriage should be viewed, not as fulfilling a desire, but as an opportunity for inner growth and development.

3. Marriage should be made an ever-creative experience.

4. Marriage is not, in itself, a solution. It simply provides new opportunities for finding solutions to life's problems.

5. Life's true fulfillments are never static. The greater the fulfillment in marriage, the more it will point a direction toward heights as yet unexplored.

6. Perfection in marriage should be seen as continuous movement in a forever-unfolding direction.

Chapter  Two

The Need for Expansiveness

There are two currents of energy and consciousness in life. One of them is expansive; the other, contractive. Heraclitus, the ancient Greek philosopher, said it well for all time: "All is flux."

As the ocean tides rise and fall, so does life fluctuate between expansion and contraction. Sometimes both currents operate simultaneously. The expansiveness of success, for example, may be offset by illness and a contraction of energy. The flowering of wisdom may be dulled by the infirmities of old age, or rendered unfruitful by obligatory retirement.

Life, though infinitely more complex than the ocean tides, resembles them in its constant expansion and contraction. While we cannot safely ignore these currents, we can, with a little wisdom, turn them to good advantage. The very contraction of physical energy during illness, for example, imposed by outward inaction, can be turned to advantage by redirecting that energy toward increasing our knowledge and understanding. The very fact of forced retirement, due to old age, can inspire us to redirect our energy into other, more creative, channels: into painting, perhaps, or writing, or counseling others who are still plodding along on the "nine-to-five" treadmill.

There are aspects, in other words, of the dual currents of expansion and contraction that are subject to the control of human will. Outer realities cannot always be changed, but we can always determine our *reaction* to them.

Marriage, like life itself, and like all human relationships, has its ups and downs. Today's expansion, whether of outer success or of inner feelings of love or happiness, inevitably alternates with its opposite, for such is the ineluctable flow of things. What can couples do but accept it? Only thus can they make the best of it. This "best" is determined by how intelligently a person reacts to whatever happens.

The most loving exchange may give way suddenly to a mood shift. What does one do when one's partner swings unexpectedly from laughter to tears, or from tender smiles to anger and scorn? The normal human reaction is to respond contractively: to withdraw within, to feel hurt—or else, to retaliate in kind.

To strike back is to force both partners into the flow of contractive energy. As long as only one partner succumbs to this current, the other may be able to lift them both out of the contractive stream. Once both enter it, however, nothing can be done but wait for the tides to change—in a day, a week, or—years? When both partners in a marriage become contractive, they are like the south poles of a magnet in close proximity to each other: They repel each other instead of increasing the natural magnetism between them.

◈ The Danger of Contractiveness ◈

Marriage is also threatened from without. Today's success may easily become tomorrow's failure. What can couples do, when such a shift occurs? If they react negatively—not toward one another, but against the world—they create an even worse plight for themselves. It is sad for marriage to end in divorce, but it is tragic when a shared contractiveness results in a couple divorcing themselves from objective reality. For in this case their contractiveness only becomes compounded.

When couples withdraw from each other, their marriage is weakened, if not threatened. But when, in unison, they withdraw from outer challenges to their happiness, they strengthen the bond they share by emphasizing its contractive, not its expansive, aspects. They thereby weaken their ability to deal creatively with life itself. Marriage in this case, instead of helping them to grow, poses a definite obstacle to growth.

Expansion and contraction in Nature are always, like the ocean tides, neutral. Not so, the tides of expansion and contraction in human nature. We can—we *must*—rise above the contractive tides and swim energetically with the expansive, for thereon depend our continuing growth and lasting happiness. An expansive outlook is accompanied by an inner sense of fulfillment. A contractive consciousness is accompanied by misery and bitterness.

Why is this so? I think it is because contractiveness separates us from a greater reality to which we instinctively know that we belong. Ego-consciousness it is which causes us mentally to separate ourselves from that reality. Poetic souls who lament their "aloneness" in the universe are really only lamenting the intensity of their self-involvement. Jean Paul Sartre, in writing, "To be conscious of another is to be conscious of what one is not," was simply betraying his ego-addiction; he was not displaying any philosophical depth. All of us are, in truth, integral parts of all that IS. Like waves on the ocean, our egos are simply protrusions of Infinite Reality.

In this sense, there is something in all of us that seeks to reach out toward, to embrace, that reality. We feel fulfilled to the extent that we succeed in doing so. And we feel cheated of fulfillment to the extent that we withdraw into ourselves, rejecting that reality.

The contraction and expansion that Nature imposes from without is inevitable. *Our own* contraction or expansion of consciousness, on the other hand, is determined not by objective Nature, but by ourselves. By the way we react *in ourselves* to external circumstances, we determine whether our lives will flow with the upward, integrative, expansive process of evolution, or accompany Nature's downward, devolutionary process toward contraction and disintegration.

❧ "Us Four and No More" ❧

Marriage itself ought to be an integrative, expansive process: a uniting of two souls; an invitation to other souls to enter this process as children. If, however, this expansive union subsequently turns into an affirmation of separateness from everyone outside the family unit, it actually results in an over-all process of contraction, and of disintegration.

Contraction, or devolution, as a mental attitude, works against the deepest impulse of human nature, which is ever toward self-expansion. As this attitude draws energies and perceptions inward upon the ego, its effect is to isolate one. A contractive attitude is degenerative because it denotes a rejection of life's challenges, and an attempt to meet them self-protectively. The result is a sense of diminishing self-identity.

An inward contraction upon the ego always brings with it a sense of loss, of suffering and pain—the consequences of mental and spiritual suffocation. Marriage is wholesome only when the expansiveness it was designed to promote continues outward to embrace the world. Otherwise, couples, by limiting their sympathies to one another, become psychically ingrown. Like binary stars, the centripetal force of their egos' magnetism becomes only strengthened.

Contraction and expansion must be understood as *directions* only, not as fixed realities. At no point is it legitimate to say, "I'm expanded at last"; or to denounce someone as "utterly contractive!" Soul-evolution, unlike the human body, never reaches the point of maximum growth.

An "us four and no more" consciousness is only delusively expansive. Ultimately, it reinforces the very vortex of egoic energy from which it has treacherously promised an escape. It creates a cozy nest, psychologically, where littleness is exalted to the level of a principle, and the bright intelligence of one's early years withers gradually into the muttering querulousness of old age.

An expansive attitude, on the contrary, generates an expansion of *self*-awareness: a growing sense of identity that includes a much greater reality. This, partly, is what makes marriage and family such an important human institution. For by inviting people to include others' well-being in their own, it encourages them to establish an outward direction of sympathy, an expansion of self-awareness.

Selfishness—though rationalized in the name of self-fulfillment—has the very opposite effect: It narrows our parameters. As the heart's sympathies shrink inward, they, in a very real sense, squeeze the heart dry and make it barren and hard. Hardheartedness diminishes our ability to feel sympathy toward others, and ultimately even toward ourselves. Losing the ability to feel, we experience only intense inner suffering.

Generosity has the self-fulfilling effect of softening the heart. Only with softened feelings can we achieve what we truly want in life: an expansion of inner joy.

These are simple facts of life. They are universal, and not matters of personal taste, opinion, or religious belief.

❧ The Purpose of Marriage ❧

Marriage, to be fulfilling, must not shut mental windows upon the world: It must open them in a spirit of kinship with all life. When couples love each other in a spirit of giving, not of taking, they strengthen each other. In this increased strength, they discover a natural need to embrace the world lovingly, without fear, secure in their sense of *belonging* to one another and, through each other, to the universe.

Truly to love one's marriage partner means not to limit that love narrowly to him, or to her, but gradually to broaden love itself until it is realized as a Universal Truth.

Marriage, in the greater scheme of things, was never meant to be a "closed corporation." It was meant to expand our consciousness from the narrow confines of self-love, that we be inspired ultimately to embrace universal, divine love.

⚘ Points to Remember ⚘

1. There are two currents that operate constantly in life: the one is expansive; the other, contractive.

2. While we cannot control these currents outwardly, we *can* determine our reaction to them, and thereby turn them to good advantage.

3. An expansive reaction is accompanied by an inner sense of fulfillment. A contractive reaction is accompanied by misery and bitterness.

4. We find fulfillment in life to the extent that we succeed in reaching out toward and embracing a larger reality than ourselves.

5. Marriage is truly rewarding when the self-expansion it was designed to promote continues outward to include the world.

6. Contraction and expansion must be understood as *directions* only, not as fixed states of being.

7. An expansive attitude generates an expansion of *self*-awareness.

8. Generosity has the self-fulfilling effect of softening the heart. Only with softened feelings can we achieve what we truly want in life: an expansion of inner joy.

9. Marriage, to be fulfilling, must open mental windows upon the world in a spirit of kinship with all life.

10. Truly to love one's marriage partner means gradually to broaden that love until it becomes universal.

Chapter  Three

Why Marriage?

There is a story of a sculptor in India who was asked by an admirer how he had managed to capture so perfectly in stone the shape of an elephant.

"It was easy," replied the artist. "I simply chiseled away everything that didn't look like an elephant."

Marriage ought to be approached in a similar spirit. For if one is ever truly to find happiness in marriage, one must be self-honest. Every selfish desire must be recognized for the "black hole" it is, and rigidly excluded. Every contractive expectation must be caught the moment it enters the mind, and eliminated.

Unfortunately, society encourages selfishness by emphasizing the gratifications of marriage, not its obligations. The consequence, all too often, is tragedy.

It was fear of this tragedy that caused a couple, friends of mine, to reject marriage altogether. When I proposed to them that they marry (they'd been living together for years), they told me they'd seen too many of their friends, after years spent loyally together, break up once they'd solemnized their union with wedding vows.

I was astonished. Why? I asked. The couple put it this way: Their friends, after marriage, had formed different expectations of one another, based on what they thought marriage was *supposed* to mean. They "bought into" a cultural mythology. Both found themselves thinking, for instance, in terms of what their partner *owed* them. Beforehand, their union had been based on a spirit of mutual freedom. Now, it was based on what they could gain from one another.

We see here again how important it is that marriage be *expansive*. The self-giving implicit in getting married ought not to give rise, though it often does, to bargaining attitudes that would be more appropriate in an oriental bazaar. The attention shifts from "How much can I give?" to "How much can I get out of this arrangement?"

I told my friends I thought they were mistaken in blaming the institution of marriage itself, that the fault lay in false notions of what marriage ought to mean.

Marriage, to be successful, must be based on a free sharing, not on a mutual sense of obligation. Obligation can be made another word for bondage. When married people look at each other with the thought, "What's in it for me?" love flies out the window. Unfortunately, people are not even raised to think expansively. There is, rather, a growing tendency in society these days to think in terms of what the world *owes* us, rather than what each of us, personally, can do for others, and for the world, to make it a better place to live in.

It is time classes were offered to children, as early as junior high school, on how to live a fulfilled and happy life. Subjects taught could include how to create happy and harmonious marriages. Wouldn't such a teaching touch more closely on the true needs of children as they approach adulthood, than, say, medieval history?

So convinced am I of the importance of this concept that I've written a book on it, titled *Education for Life*, suggesting ways to prepare children for the challenges of life. This book offers a system of teaching that includes more than the standard subjects—"readin', writin', an' 'rithmetic." The system offers instruction also in how to live life for one's own, and for others', highest happiness and well-being.

❧ The Common Confusion ❧

People stumble into marriage—almost accidentally. They confuse matrimony with mood images, and surround those mental images with dim candlelight and soft music. If thoughts of dirty diapers, unpaid bills, and mutually conflicting desires intrude at all into this romantic dream, they come filtered by moonlight and angel choirs. Every cloud over the blissful couple's future happiness is visualized as being dispersed by a smile; every sob, as being transformed into a cheerful song; every discord, as being resolved in a perfect harmony.

Was it George Bernard Shaw who said, of youth's expectation that romantic love will be permanent, "I cannot imagine people even *wanting* such a debilitating emotion to last forever!"

It is unrealistic to expect love, considered purely as an emotion, to continue unchanged through years of married life—unrefined, and therefore undeveloped. The soul is capable of much deeper feelings, feelings that soar to the very heights of divine love. Even spiritual love has commonly proved, in the lives of mystics, a flame difficult to keep constantly burning. Mystical literature refers frequently to "dry periods," when the soul, though longing for constancy in devotion, feels bereft of love's sweetness.

If dryness can occur in a saint's relationship with God, how much more so is it bound to occur in the fluctuations of feeling that are normal to male and female relationships.

❧ Removing the Mists ❧

It seems obvious, if we want to view marriage as it is, and not veiled in imaginary mists—that we must think of it as normal to the human condition, not as a special condition separate from normal life. What it takes, in other words, to become a successful human being is essentially what it takes to become a successful marriage partner.

Romantics will, of course, disagree with me. They will allude to those particular features—beauty, for example, or (heaven help them) a dimpled smile—in members of the opposite sex which attract them to certain people as possible marriage partners whom they wouldn't dream of hiring as business partners. And of course I'd be mad to argue with them. All I'm saying is that the real *basis* of a successful marriage is not sex appeal, but those simple, human considerations which make for happy unions of all kinds—yes, even business partnerships.

For those persons, especially, who aspire to increase their understanding, marriage should be viewed as a doorway to self-expansion. The increase sought should include above all a *spiritual* dimension. For the basic purpose of marriage is not to enroll two egos in a "mutual admiration society." And it certainly is not merely to propagate the species. It is to contribute to the fundamental purpose of life, which is to expand the limitations of human consciousness toward universal awareness.

❧ The Quest for Higher Values ❧

Human beings, let it be emphasized, are more than biological animals. It would seem almost ridiculous to make this statement were it not one of the tenets—*superstitions* might be a better word—of our times that human beings are merely that: that their behavior is motivated entirely by animal urges. Increasing numbers of people, fortunately, are becoming dissatisfied with that definition. They are beginning to suspect that human life is worthwhile, really, only to the extent that it includes a quest for higher values in the broad quest for fulfillment. In short, we have souls—or say, rather, we *are* souls—and we must therefore seek gratification for spiritual hungers also.

Each of us was born with twin hungers: for wisdom, and for selfless love. Each of us also longs in his soul for perfect joy. No human activity is fully satisfying that fails to take these needs into consideration.

Were the only purpose of marriage to propagate the species, that fact alone would exclude couples that are unable to bear children. Is their marriage invalid because it is biologically fruitless? Surely not! Marriage can be fruitful in ways that have nothing to do with biology.

What, then, are those ways? I have mentioned that marriage can help people to break the narrow confines of selfishness and egoism. By learning to embrace a larger reality than their own, they can break the hard shell of self-involvement that holds humanity prisoner.

Marriage can also help people expand their consciousness by balancing those fundamental aspects of human nature: feeling, and reason. When feeling and reason are balanced and refined, the result is a combination of love and wisdom, which are salient attributes of God.

A further purpose of marriage is self-knowledge and self-understanding. Living in close proximity to another human being affords an objective proving ground for personal development. For it is relatively easy to be gracious, kind, and forgiving to chance acquaintances, but only in the close quarters of constant, daily association is our caliber really tested.

❧ Points to Remember ❧

1. Every selfish desire in marriage must be recognized as unproductive, because contractive, and must be rigidly excluded.

2. Marriage, to be successful, must be based on a free sharing, not on a mutual sense of obligation.

3. Marriage must not be confused with mood images.

4. The real *basis* of a successful marriage is not so much sex appeal as those simple human considerations—kindness, for example, and courtesy—which make for happy unions of all kinds.

5. The expansion sought in marriage should include, above all, a spiritual dimension.

6. Marriage contributes toward the fundamental purpose of life itself: to expand the limitations of human consciousness toward universal awareness.

7. Each of us was born with a hunger for wisdom, for selfless love, for perfect joy. No human activity is fully satisfactory that fails to take these abiding needs into consideration.

8. A basic purpose of marriage is the opportunity it provides for self-knowledge, for self-understanding.

Chapter Four

"You Just Don't Understand"

The heading of this chapter is taken from the title of an interesting book by Deborah Tannen, PH.D., concerning the differences between men and women.

Many people in modern times insist that these differences don't exist, except biologically; that it is our conditioning from early childhood that produces different patterns of behavior.

Do you really believe that? I wouldn't contest that on some deep level of our being—as souls, let us say—we are one, and therefore no different from one another. Nor would I contest that our upbringing, and society's expectations of us, condition our behavior. But common experience tells us, surely, that innate differences do exist. Even boy and girl babies behave differently from one another. To claim otherwise would be to try to squeeze reality into a box of intellectual theory, as people do who base their beliefs on what they think *ought* to be, not on what *is*.

Dr. Spock, the famous baby doctor, reported that, whenever he leaned down with a mirror on his forehead to examine girl babies, they would look up happily, enjoying the images reflected in the glass. But when he leaned down to examine boy babies, they would reach up and grasp his mirror as if trying to figure out what it was and how it worked.

At this point, some of my women readers may protest, "But I, too, like to figure things out and discover how they work! I don't only enjoy their beauty." Well, if so, then perhaps I, as a man, ought to protest with equal vehemence, "But I, too, love beauty. I don't only want to figure out how things work." In fact, one of my most precious memories as a child is a mirror—Dr. Spock's very example—that my mother kept on her dresser. It had a beveled edge, and I would gaze into it for what, from this point in time, seems like hours, enjoying the rainbow colors while I imagined myself living in a land of radiant light. The only thing of my mother's that I requested after her death was that very mirror. My sisters-in-law were puzzled, but willing to gratify my whim. And there sits the mirror in my bedroom—never used, but often enjoyed.

So—both the women and the men in the crowd can be upset with Dr. Spock, if we like. But the "good" doctor (why does convention seem always to label doctors "good"?) was simply reporting a personal observation, and an interesting one. I, for one, am willing to consider its implications. Is my willingness simply the masculine influence on my nature?

No, girls don't *have* to limit themselves to a love for beauty; they don't *have* to be uninterested in the way things work. They don't *have* to be anything they don't want to be. In fact, there are women I know who, without being in any way unfeminine, are excellent mechanics. To me, on the other hand, a car is a magic totem. I propitiate the motor by turning the key. If the motor is pleased, it turns over and I'm free to begin my journey. If it is not pleased, the only thing I can think of to do is get out and kick a tire—or, if there's a telephone nearby (I have a bit of a phobia against telephones, too), phone the AAA.

My own interest in how things work finds its outlet more in a lifelong fascination with the intricacies of life and of human nature: with why people are the way they are, why they do the things they do, and how to help them to find true happiness in their lives.

So—we're all different, and the world is much the richer for our differences. Nevertheless, there *are* influences in our lives, and sex is, undeniably, one of them. We can, if we so choose, rise above any influence, including that of sex. But not to admit that the sex into which we were born affects our outlook on life is to give that influence even more power over us—the power that reality always exerts over ignorance.

It is like the story of three men who died and went to hell. They had been faithful churchgoers, and couldn't understand why they'd ended up in the wrong place. One of them, a former Roman Catholic, said, "I must have missed mass one Sunday." The second one, a former Baptist, said, "Perhaps I wasn't fully immersed when I was baptized." At that point they turned to the third of them, a former Christian Scientist, and asked, "So how come you're here?"

"Oh," he replied, "but I'm not!"

In the case of these men, to be sure, it didn't really matter, since they were stuck in That Place anyway. But what of people in situations where the possibility exists for them to improve matters? To say, "There's nothing to be improved," will prevent them from even making the attempt.

There are many women who define themselves too narrowly by their womanhood, simply because they don't realize that they're defining themselves at all. And there are many men who cannot see beyond their "macho" self-image for the same reason.

Paramhansa Yogananda related the story of a conversation he'd had once with a woman novelist who prided herself on her powers of impersonal reasoning. Well, of course, to be a woman doesn't incapacitate one, rationally! What this woman said, however, was, "I go *only* by reason."

Yogananda tactfully refrained from making a direct response. Instead, cautiously, he steered the conversation around to the subject of a certain other woman novelist. Once this new subject had been clearly defined, his companion reacted vigorously by lambasting her "rival."

"So you go only by reason, do you?" queried Yogananda, smiling. The woman had little choice at that point but to laugh with him, admitting that she'd given herself away.

❧ Reason and Feeling ❧

In men, said Yogananda, reason is uppermost; feeling is kept hidden. In women, feeling is uppermost; reason is kept hidden. These differences in no way indicate that men haven't as great a *capacity* for feeling, or women as great a *capacity* for reason. A specific man may be capable of deeper feeling, and greater love, than most women; and a specific woman may be capable of reasoning more clearly than most men. Each of these, however, *in his own nature*, is likely to depend more on reason, if a man, and more on feeling, if a woman.

It is only in saints that we find these two attributes perfectly balanced. Paramhansa Yogananda was as much a mother to his disciples as a father. St. Teresa of Avila was once described by a city official, to whom she'd gone to solicit his help in a matter pertaining to her convent, as, "No nun, but a bearded man!"

As we perfect ourselves, inwardly, we achieve a perfect balance between reason and feeling, and between wisdom and love. Men become kinder, more compassionate; women become more reasonable, less emotional.

Reason, without feeling, loses touch with the unitive power of intuition. Becoming over-analytical, it dissects endlessly until the very life in whatever it is analyzing is destroyed.

Feeling, on the other hand, when it is not guided by reason, falls into a welter of emotions.

Calm feeling *is* intuition. That is why women are often more intuitive than men. When feeling becomes agitated, however, or excited, it creates emotional waves that distort mental vision, causing a person to lose touch with objective reality.

No matter how convinced a person is of the validity of his perceptions, if emotion rules, they are not to be trusted. Reason itself is guided by feeling, but *mis*guided by emotion. A person suffering from moods, for example, will find every reason in the world to justify those moods.

Feeling must be kept in a state of calm reason. Reason must be inspired by calm feeling. Thus do love and wisdom flower together in human consciousness.

All human beings yearn, at least subconsciously, to achieve this inner balance between their feeling and their reasoning natures. Without such a balance, they never find fulfillment.

This is the deeper reason why men and women are instinctively attracted to each other. The attraction is far more than physical: It is born of the desire to balance, each in oneself, the feeling and reasoning natures. The more fully this inner balance is achieved, the less need is there to affirm it outwardly, in physical union or in marriage. The longing develops, then, for soul-union with the Divine.

❧ "The War between the Sexes" ❧

Long before the antagonism between the sexes developed to its present level of notoriety, people were already talking—more in amusement, then, than in anger—about "the battle of the sexes." Nowadays, that battle has escalated into outright war. Feminist groups accuse men unilaterally of so many crimes that men are still reeling under their blows. Inevitably, in time, those men who feel injured will rally, and retaliate. For such is human nature.

Jesus Christ put it perfectly when he said, "Whosoever takes up the sword shall perish by the sword." The greater the wave of ego at the surface of life's sea, the more mightily it will crash against other waves that have pushed themselves high also in their self-esteem. In the present instance, the retaliation will, I imagine, take rather the form of indifference than of counter-accusations. If so, this may prove a bitter pill indeed for those who have accustomed themselves to shouting accusations in anger.

I saw a headline recently on the cover of a national magazine; it asked the question: "Are men really that bad?" And I thought, "For feminists to accuse men *in toto* is like one side of a coin accusing the other of being made of debased metal." We're all the same species, after all.

To accuse others, moreover, especially in anger, is an all-but-certain sign that the faults one perceives in them already exist in oneself. For ego is like colored glass: It taints everything that the mind views. This, again, is a simple fact of human nature. By sympathy, and still more by empathy—like a piano, which resonates with other notes—understanding comes. Only by kindness and generosity can we achieve true insight into others—and into our own selves.

What gain is there in viewing anything one-sidedly? What do women gain by trying to be as masculine as men? The shoe, so far, has not yet come onto the other foot, but it might easily do so: Could men be as good at being feminine as women are? Even were both sides to prove their points, where would be the advantage? Balance cannot be achieved by renouncing one side of *anything* for its opposite.

⚘ Vive La Difference ⚘

What is needed, and what matrimony can help people to achieve, is *appreciation*, not warfare, between the sexes. For each has something to give that the other needs, for proper balance.

Individuals will always display idiosyncrasies. In their totality, people no doubt span the entire spectrum of human potential. (I remember a friend of mine commenting on a woman he'd just met: "She has enough male hormones for the entire Rams football team!") Variety contributes to the richness and color of life's tapestry.

For anyone to state, however, "This is how all women *ought* to be," or, "This is how every man *ought* to be," is to fly in the face of reality, and to place an intolerable burden on those who want simply to be themselves.

I once asked an interior decorator to help me in choosing fabrics for my living room. She showed me an assortment of browns and grays.

"Why have you selected those colors?" I asked.

"Well, these are masculine colors."

"And why," I protested, "should I limit myself to masculine colors? Show me things that are *beautiful*! I'd rather choose colors that resonate with something more expansive than my masculinity. I *am* a man; what more can be said on the subject? I'd rather emphasize my *humanity*."

To repeat my earlier point, this isn't to say that instinctive differences don't exist. Women generally, for instance, like lace and knick-knacks; men generally prefer a more Spartan line, and fewer ornaments. It isn't that one is better than the other, or even more beautiful. Good taste in these matters is entirely subjective; it may depend simply on a difference in hormones.

Women tend to like softness, suggestive of tender feelings. Men tend to prefer clean, sweeping lines, suggestive of boldness and courage.

Women have a fondness for little *objets d'art*, perhaps because feminine nature is so adept at observing and focusing on the details of a situation. Men prefer rooms that they themselves would define as "uncluttered," perhaps because masculine nature is more inclined to concentrate on the over-all picture.

Who is to say which is better? Balance is necessary for complete insight in any situation.

Most women, again, find nothing attractive in the thought of battling their way up the corporate ladder. As Deborah Tannen puts it in her book, *You Just Don't Understand*, women generally are more interested in bonding with others. She was mistaken, however, in her subsequent statement that men, by contrast, are egotistically, even ruthlessly, competitive. Granting that many men *are* motivated by competition, women often make the error of equating the drive for accomplishment (which is often simply a quest for perfection) with ego, and the lack of such a drive with an absence of ego. To claim, moreover, that women lack the competitive instinct is to fly in the face of a vast quantity of conventional wisdom.

Neither competition nor bonding can explain the truly great accomplishments of the human race: the great discoveries of science, the great works of art, the heroic deeds of self-denial and self-sacrifice.

Ego, considered as a flaw (rather than the "leg up" the ladder of evolution that it provides humanity), is simply exaggerated self-involvement. Ego is a human reality; it is no more pronounced in one sex than in the other. It merely manifests differently in the two sexes, and in different individuals. To be self-effacing or insecure (typical feminine weaknesses) can be as much an expression of exaggerated self-consciousness as to be aggressive or over-confident (typical masculine failings).

Insecurity, like a sponge, sucks energy into itself; little energy is free to escape. Over-confidence, on the other hand, squeezes the sponge dry of life-giving energy, leaving anything that it accomplishes dry and uninspired.

Typical feminine manifestations of ego are transcended by nurturing others. Typical masculine manifestations are transcended by creativity in both action and thought, with growing awareness that the true source of creative inspiration is not the ego, but Truth itself.

Suppression of the nurturing instinct leads to dryness of heart, and a deep sense of unfulfillment. Suppression of the creative urge leads to a festering sense of frustration.

Balance is achieved, on the one side, by nurturing others in such a way as not to keep them dependent on you for their nurturing, but to make them complete and independent in themselves. Balance is achieved, on the other side, by offering, through one's creative energy and thoughts, inspiration and nourishment to all.

It is time, I think, to abandon the fruitless debate as to the relative *merits* of men and women, and to recognize that the qualities expressed by each are equally necessary to the complete human being.

Which side of a coin is *better* than the other? Without both sides, there would be no coin! There is a need in human nature for conquest and achievement. And there is a need also to project energy outward in ways that are nourishing and healing.

ꙮ Women in Today's World ꙮ

Granting the need in the present-day economy for husband and wife to work, how will things arrange themselves once prosperity comes and further income ceases to be a pressing need? It is good in a marriage, surely, for one partner to concentrate on providing prosperity for the home, while the other is devoted to *creating* a home—not a house, merely, where two roommates meet at supper and at bedtime. There is a need to complement the outward flow of energy with an inner regeneration of energy. As the ocean tides ebb and flow, so also does energy. Human nature cannot remain long fulfilled if it flows only in one direction.

What, then, about women in business? in politics? in public positions of all kinds? Are they out of place? Is woman's place, as so many (including not a few women) insist, in the home? Were I a woman, I'd be in there with the feminists, answering as politely as I could, "Don't tell me how to live my life!" I choose to act as I feel inspired to do from within, not as others, even from the best of motives, tell me I should.

There are, I believe, greater currents involved here than most people realize. Women are coming to the fore in every field for reasons that have less to do with their individual desires than with the needs of the human race as a whole. The issue concerns not so much their own fulfillment as a universal need for balance. The life-force within us ever propels the human race toward equilibrium.

Women nowadays (speaking, again, generally) feel impelled from within to help bring about this balance. Their active participation in business, in politics, and in public positions of all kinds is vitally needed, and has proved greatly beneficial.

In the business world, a need exists for the expression of heart qualities—concern for others, support for one's fellow workers, consideration for the customers and for the public welfare in general.

In politics, there is a desperate need for genuine (not postured) cooperation: for a spirit born not of the drive for power, but of real concern and fellow-feeling for humanity as a whole.

Women's presence in commerce and politics, and in public affairs generally, is also needed in order to demonstrate feminine competence in fields where men have, for centuries, held a monopoly.

It is not entirely fair for women to hurl accusations of "male chauvinism" at men who, in the past, have questioned their competence in these fields. The simple fact is, when an ability has not been demonstrated, it is commonly assumed to be absent. Women make the same assumptions about men, and for the same reasons. (Have you never heard a woman's condescending chuckle, when a man picks up thread and needle to sew on a button?)

Where the family is concerned, history has arranged matters in such a way that man, generally, has been the bread winner, and woman, the home maker. Economic necessity has often forced both to work; as that need diminishes, however, the tendency seems to have been to return to the traditional division of responsibilities. If this situation should change drastically in future—well, it will be interesting to see how the change comes about.

There is one change for which there will definitely be a need: Women may, generally speaking, find greater fulfillment in the creation of a harmonious home than in the battle of the marketplace. Intelligent women, however, and well-educated women especially, cannot remain satisfied for long on a daily diet of nothing but baby talk. They want challenges for their minds and for their spirits. They want the opportunity to deepen their feeling natures, their intuition, their instinct for offering nourishment not only in the form of milk, but of wholesome, even crusading, energy and of deep intuition. It is, I think, no accident of nature that a woman's breasts, unlike those in females of the lower species, are located in the region of the heart, whence (in the neural center of the spine opposite the heart) emanate feelings of kindness, empathy, and love.

✺ Women as Uplifters ✹ of Consciousness

Women can help to fulfill a need that, so far, has yet to be fully recognized: to improve the *quality* of life on the planet—to look beyond the narrow confines of home and family and inspire people to consider the whole world as their home, and the whole human race as their family.

It is women, primarily—speaking, again, generally; there is no other way to speak of such matters—who always have been and probably always will be designated by Nature to uplift the human race, by reminding humanity of its highest potentials. Without this contribution, whatever the source, the human race will not long remain "the noblest of the animals." Therefore it is that the Hindu scripture, the *Bhagavad Gita*, warns that when women lose their sense of values, society perishes.

It is a pity so many women feel that, in order to succeed in outward roles, they must behave like men. . . . Well, but why fret or become overly concerned in these matters? Life itself—the great balancer—will doubtless inspire women in its own time to recognize once again their special mission.

The basic point of this chapter is this: that feeling and reason, both, are important, and both equally so. Women and men therefore need to learn to live in harmony together, with ever-deepening appreciation for those qualities in each other which complement their own. Only by mutual respect and appreciation can marriage become truly a delight. And only by mutual respect and appreciation can marriage also give its participants the opportunity for mutual growth, which is its highest potential.

Married couples would do well to evaluate marriage from a point of view of self-expansion. It is time people stopped depending on outmoded social definitions of marriage. Like the sculptor of the elephant described in the last chapter, couples should chip away from their notions of marriage anything that is not compatible with their higher aspirations.

The romantically inclined should view marriage, not as an end in itself, but as a *direction*. Couples should realize that the deeper purpose behind their union is the opportunity it gives them for development toward the higher goal of *perfect* union, a goal essentially the same for all mankind: union with God.

☙ **Points to Remember** ☙

1. We're all different, and the world is much the richer for our differences.

2. In men, reason is uppermost; feeling is kept hidden. In women, feeling is uppermost; reason is kept hidden.

3. As we perfect ourselves, inwardly, we achieve a perfect balance between reason and feeling, and between wisdom and love. Men become kinder, more compassionate; women become more reasonable, less emotional.

4. Feeling must be kept in a state of reason. Reason must be inspired by calm feeling. Thus do love and wisdom flower together in human consciousness.

5. The recognition of the need for balancing feeling and reason is the deeper reason why men and women are instinctively attracted to each other.

6. To accuse others, especially in anger, is an all-but-certain sign that the faults one perceives in them already exist in oneself. Ego is a colored glass that taints everything viewed by the mind.

7. Only by kindness and a generous spirit can we achieve true insight into other human beings—and into our own selves.

8. What is needed, and what matrimony can help people to achieve, is *appreciation*, not warfare, between the sexes.

9. Typical feminine manifestations of the ego are transcended by nurturing others. Typical masculine manifestations are transcended by creativity.

10. Women are coming to the fore in every field for reasons that have less to do with their individual desires than with the needs of the human race as a whole.

11. Woman can help to fulfill a need that, so far, has yet to be fully recognized—to improve the *quality* of life on the planet.

12. Married couples would do well to evaluate marriage from a point of view of self-expansion.

13. Couples should realize that the deeper purpose behind their union is the opportunity it gives them for development toward the higher goal of spiritual union.

Chapter  Five

Intuition

Some years ago I parked my car on a street in Florence, Italy—illegally, as it turned out. When I returned to the car, I found a letter on the windshield from the police.

"*Egregio Signore*," it began.

"*Egregio*?" I thought. *Egregious*, in English, means "outstandingly bad." Surely they couldn't be adding insult to their injury of a fine! I was momentarily comforted by the reflection that the police would never be able to trace me: I'd rented the car in Austria. My confidence increased on reflection that, probably, Italy's extradition treaties didn't extend to parking tickets.

The Florentine police had evidently reached the same conclusions, for the envelope proved to contain nothing more than their letter.

So, then, were they getting back at me with that "*Egregio*"?

Fumbling through my Italian-English dictionary, I discovered that *egregio* is an honorific; it means, simply, "distinguished." All they'd called me was, "Distinguished Sir."

Linguistic cousins of this sort are known as "friendly enemies": words with the same roots, but often with quite opposite meanings. *Egregio* and "egregious" both have their origin in Latin: *ex gregius*—"out of the herd." In English, also, *egregious* originally meant "distinguished." Language evolves, however. I imagine that in time the word came to mean "different," and from there slipped just a little further to its present meaning, "outstandingly bad." When meanings change in language, they seem generally to change for the worse—like our word *knave*, which originally meant, simply, *boy*.

"Out of the herd." There *does* seem to be a tendency in human nature to judge those who are different from the norm to be worse, not better, than other people.

Back to the subject of this book: Men have long disparaged women for no better reason than that they simply aren't men. And women, too, have long dismissed anything men say or do with the mere epithet: "Men!"

Men: "Bah—Women drivers!"

Women: "Bah—Male animal!"

Men: "Bah—Feminine intuition!"

Women: "Bah—Male chauvinist!"

I once was driving in Rome, during another visit to Italy, in a car I'd bought in Naples—"Napoli," as the Italians call it. The license plate contained the letters *NA*, for Napoli. Behind me, another driver in that rush-hour traffic, seeing the license plate and convinced that I was deliberately blocking his way, shouted at me, "Napoli!" For him, no more elaborate insult was required.

In Napoli, of course, and in every other Italian city, similar epithets are used to denigrate people from any other city than one's own. In Italy it is sufficient for someone to come from anywhere else to be branded eccentric. The first time that all Italians viewed themselves as Italians in spirit, rather than as Napoletani or Romani or Fiorentini, was on the occasion, several years ago, when Italy won the World Cup in soccer.

I hope I haven't taken too much time in getting to the real substance of this chapter. A little humor can't hurt, surely, when the subject concerns something about which people nowadays are so grimly in earnest that one almost trembles to speak, fearing lest he inadvertently offend against some festering sensibility, or commit the inadmissible crime of political incorrectness.

The French have an apt saying, "*Vive la difference!*" We should be thankful for the myriads of differences in human nature. If they didn't exist—if everyone in the choir, for example, were a tenor—imagine how uninteresting life's harmonies would be.

The need for variety is especially true as regards the differences between men and women. Were these differences somehow to be abolished, human nature would become as flat-tasting as wilted lettuce.

Let us look at that oft-heard expression of masculine contempt: "Bah—feminine intuition!" Women *are* often, in fact, intuitive. So also, though generally in other ways, are men.

Women's intuition finds expression most often through their insights into people. A wife may warn her husband, for instance, "That person you've been thinking of hiring isn't a good choice."

"What makes you think so?" demands the husband. "You've met him only once. The two of you have hardly exchanged three sentences!"

"Our verbal exchanges have nothing to do with it," she replies. "It's an inner feeling I have."

"Feeling!" exclaims her husband impatiently. "Can't you explain yourself *reasonably*?"

And so the husband ignores her advice. A year later, the new employee absconds with half the company's funds.

Feminine intuition. When it works, it really does work. *How* does it work? Ask, rather, how intuition itself works, not just feminine intuition.

Briefly, it works because all of us, as I mentioned in an earlier chapter, are parts of a greater reality. We appear separate from it only to the extent that we hold ourselves mentally aloof. The reason for our aloofness is ego-consciousness. When ego-consciousness subsides with a reduction of ego-driven desires and ambitions, a measure of detachment is attained from sensory awareness. Calmness then ensues. The result of calmness is a glimpse—fleetingly, at first—of the flow of things in the great stream of life all around us.

We may sense, then, a subtle connection with other people and with objective events. And we may *know*, beyond a shadow of a doubt, the truth of things beyond our sensory ken. We may understand others' deeper motivations, and the proper course to follow in our future actions.

⚛ Developing Intuition ⚛

Because reason is analytical, it separates. Reason asks, "How does *this* differ from *that?*" In this analyzing process, it cuts itself off from awareness of life's underlying oneness.

Feeling, on the other hand, reaches out instinctively to embrace life. Feeling is therefore more conscious of the underlying oneness of all things. Women, for this reason, are more often intuitive than men.

Men, too, can be intuitive, however. What they need to do is refer their reason back, for inspiration and guidance, to the feeling faculty. I say, "refer *back*" because, in the quest for understanding, the natural flow of energy is *upward*, from the heart to the head. From there the energy must flow down again to the heart—for consultation, as it were—from thence again to flow upward, thus creating a circle which gradually transforms both emotion and reason into pure feeling and clear intelligence. The result of this transformation is intuition.

The final movement of the intuitive flow is upward, through the spiritual "door" of the forehead and out into the oneness of Spirit. Thus is outer marriage perfected, finally, in inner awareness, as it becomes a marriage of the individual soul to its Eternal Source.

Men's intuition functions better, usually, in their work. A certain friend of mine was the owner of a large Christmas card factory in Detroit. He attributed his phenomenal success to an uncanny ability to know in advance which card designs people would buy, and which ones they would not. (Amusingly, my friend was Jewish.)

✌ Beyond Logic or Emotion ✌

Men often claim, after arriving at some particularly successful insight, that they achieved it by a careful process of ratiocination. They are mistaken. In truly creative reasoning there always comes a moment when the mind pauses, then makes a sudden leap, to arrive "illogically," as it seems, at the right conclusion. One simply *knows* the right answer. No further challenge on the part of reason can shake the mind's certainty. One may try, later, to explain logically how he arrived at that answer, but in fact logic could have taken him in numerous other directions. No merely logical conclusion could have given him that calm sense of certainty which he now feels. For he not only thinks it: He *knows* it. And he knows it because he *feels* it.

In such cases, a faculty beyond logic is at work: intuition.

Women often claim intuition for feelings that arise simply from their emotions, or from their likes or dislikes. It is not easy to separate emotion from calm, intuitive feeling. But the emotions, because they fluctuate constantly, can never offer a clear reflection of the realities around them, any more than the rippled surface of a lake clearly reflects the moon. Only stillness within can provide that calm certainty which is the hallmark of intuition.

The *knowing* of intuition transcends both reason and emotion: It is the perfection of both. This higher level of understanding people achieve with the marriage of feeling and reason. Intuition manifests when the emotions are calm, and when the intellect passes beyond the fluctuations of reason to a state of stillness, perfectly focused.

Feeling is the abiding reality beneath the fluctuations of emotion. Intelligence, similarly, is the abiding reality beneath the analyses of reason. Intelligent, *feeling* awareness is soul-consciousness. It is wisdom.

It is important for men and women to listen calmly to one another—for men to listen for the voice of calm feeling in women, and for women to listen for the voice of calm reason in men. For intuition—that deeper power of knowing—is what perfect marriage helps people finally to uncover in themselves.

In the individual, the heart's feeling must be directed upward, to the brain. The intelligence in the brain must turn back for inspiration to the heart. Thus, gradually, a circle is drawn that magnetically attracts expanding perceptions that reveal to the mind the oneness of all life.

If a couple want to grow deeper in understanding, the wife should offer her feelings up for consideration to the husband's impersonal logic. And the husband should draw on her intuition to direct his reasoning. If both partners are dedicated to knowing the truth, they will develop together a marvelous harmony, and an ever-expansive vision of life.

Herein lies the underlying meaning of the title of this book, *Self-Expansion Through Marriage*. For marriage can be expansive in the fullest sense only when couples use their shared perceptions to reach out intuitively toward the truth.

⚡ Points to Remember ⚡

1. Intuition works because all of us belong to a greater reality. As our ego-driven desires and ambitions subside, calmness ensues, often affording us glimpses of the flow in the greater stream of life all around us.

2. Reason is analytical; it separates. Reason asks, "How does *this* differ from *that*?" Feeling, on the other hand, reaches out instinctively to embrace life.

3. Women, because they go more by feeling, are often more intuitive than men.

4. Men, too, can be intuitive. What they must do is refer back for inspiration and guidance to the faculty of feeling.

5. In creative reasoning there comes a moment when the mind pauses, then makes a sudden leap, to arrive "illogically," as it appears, at the right conclusion. One simply *knows* the answer.

6. The *knowing* of intuition transcends both reason and emotion. It is the perfection of both.

7. Intelligent, *feeling* awareness is soul-consciousness. It is wisdom.

8. It is important for men and women to listen calmly to one another—for men to listen for the voice of calm feeling in women; for women to listen for the voice of calm reason in men.

9. Intuition—that deep power of knowing—is what perfect marriage helps people, finally, to uncover in themselves.

10. If a couple want to grow in understanding, the wife should offer her feelings up for consideration to the husband's impersonal logic. And the husband should draw on her intuition to direct his reasoning.

Chapter Six

Growing Together

My parents, when they were alive, had an unusually harmonious relationship. I never knew them to have an argument. A friend once asked my father the secret of their happiness together.

"After our wedding," my father replied with the wry humor I remember so well, "I told my wife I would make all the important decisions in our marriage." He paused a moment for dramatic effect, then added, smiling, "Since then, there haven't been any important decisions to make."

His answer was intended humorously, of course, but it also made an important point. For, needless to say, my parents did face important decisions together—some of them dramatic. Never did any of them, however, take precedence over their abiding commitment to each other.

How often in marriage—indeed, how often in all human relationships—we take the human element for granted, while focusing on some pressing project or situation. Couples even have fallings-out on how they can best improve their relationship!

A good motto in marriage, and in other relationships as well, is one I've used in various positions of leadership: *People are more important than things.*

Circumstances change, but our deeper commitments remain. They are our abiding reality.

Outsiders come and go, but those who are close to us remain—unless, indeed, we follow the example set by so many, of taking them too much for granted while treating outsiders like royalty. For many couples are gracious to the merest stranger, yet overlook the simplest courtesy to each other.

I was struck by something I read years ago. A woman had asked a certain couple, friends of hers, the formula for their marital success.

"It's really quite simple," was the reply. "We decided at the outset never to use the word, 'always,' accusingly."

How often people tell their marriage partners, "You *always* do (so and so)"; "That's how you *always* react"; or, "That's what you *always* say about him (or about her)." In such contexts, "always" is an accusation.

❧ Respect and Courtesy ❧

Marriage is a long-term investment. Even if, like a tree, it grows beyond needing that kind of care which one lavishes on a tender sapling, it nevertheless demands very special energy. Respect and consideration are the simple kindnesses in human relationships that, like oil, keep the machinery of life flowing smoothly.

A woman recently came up to me while I was seated at a table. I rose to greet her. "Hey, listen," she protested, "don't stand up. I don't want to be treated differently just because I'm a woman." My own upbringing would have had me get up for *anyone*, male or female, out of simple courtesy and respect.

But why *not* show respect to women also—as women? I can understand a woman not wanting to be treated like a china figurine. On the other hand, to treat people too casually can easily convey the message, "You have nothing I want—so, what do *you* want from me?" Lack of overt respect easily slips into its opposite: disrespect. And disrespect easily slips into rudeness.

When to be courteous, and how, and to whom, is a personal decision. To reject courtesy when it is extended, however, is to invite any of its several alternatives.

Marriage should be rooted in respect and courtesy. Without these, love never grows to become a healthy plant, capable of surviving the storms of life and of shifting fortunes. Couples who treat each other too familiarly imply, by look, word, and gesture, that there can be no further depths in the other person waiting to be explored. Such marriages have already failed.

For marriage ought to be, like life itself, an ever-expanding experience. To be so, it must be creative. Creativity implies a positive outflow of energy; lack of it implies passive receptivity to other people's energy, and to life. Passivity in marriage is like a slow-acting poison. Creativity is a tonic.

Marriage should be treated as an art. To be kept forever interesting, forever new, it must be based on giving—on loving, mutual service.

One suggestion for bringing creativity to your marriage is to try to do one thing every day that will give extra pleasure to your beloved: the gift of a flower, perhaps; a telephone call; a special smile—not with the lips, but with the eyes.

The energy in marriage is like flowing water: As long as there is creative input, it will retain its freshness. But if it remains idle for too long, the marriage will grow stagnant. Hence, again, marriage should be ever-expansive.

❧ True Soul-Union ❧

There are two ways for couples to grow together. One is by intertwining themselves, like twin creepers, until they end up so unanimous in everything that it is difficult to tell them apart—except, perhaps, by the clothes they wear. Such a relationship is suffocating, for it implies total inter-dependence, not creativity in sharing. No one, if locked in such a union, can reach out expansively toward a larger reality.

The other way for couples to grow together is by accepting the simple fact that perfect union is achieved not only physically or mentally, but above all in soul-union. Such a union cannot be forged by the tendrils of a close embrace. Nor is it formed by the mere concurrence of personal tastes and ideas. It is a union in Eternal Truth.

Perfect unity of flesh and thought is not a human possibility, if only because the flesh must die and because thoughts are only ripples of consciousness: They change, shift, and vanish constantly. The ocean waves are one only in the sense that they belong to the same ocean.

True growth in marriage is possible only if each partner assumes personal responsibility for their growth together. Conscience is an individual matter. It can easily be dulled by making it a joint responsibility, each spouse asking the other, "Well, dear, what do *you* think?"

Mutual growth is possible only from the soil of mutual respect. And respect flourishes best when a degree of distance, mutually agreed upon, is maintained. It is good, even in the intimacy of marriage, for couples to appreciate each other's need for privacy.

For everyone needs some space of his own. Couples need some time to themselves—both as a couple, and also apart from one another—that they may return to the challenges of life refreshed and with renewed enthusiasm. Only in a state of inner freedom can we preserve that creative joy which is the highest promise of any relationship.

Remember, alone you came into this world, and alone you will leave it at death. Any effort to escape this finality by clinging to another human being is founded on a profound misunderstanding of what, simply and forever, IS. Any union that encourages such a clinging is headed—like a rudderless ship—toward the rocks of disappointment and disillusionment.

I remember one couple: The wife so doted on the husband that he, unable to bear her suffocating worship, took to drinking heavily. The more she worshiped him, the harder he drank. It was painful to me, as their friend, to see them drifting toward inevitable disaster. Nor could I say whose was the greater pain: hers, for doting so fondly on someone who, by his behavior, was bound to disappoint her in the end; or his, for the imprisonment he felt, caged in an excessive dependency which he could not, by the canons of his upbringing, define as anything but desirable and good.

The fact is, her affection was possessive, and therefore far less generous than it seemed. True love is based on mutual giving. It never makes demands. Never does it say to the other person, "You *owe* me such and so, because I am your wife (or your husband)."

Love is a giving, a sharing: It is not a taking.

Marriage is such a sensitive relationship that if in any way you try to coerce your partner to follow your ways, you risk damaging your relationship irretrievably.

Respect one another's free will. Instead of issuing emotional commands and ultimatums, *offer* your suggestions kindly—even humbly—for your partner's free consideration.

A body without a head cannot function, though a headless chicken may run in circles for a time. A physical and mental "body," similarly, that lacks the direction of deeper, spiritual awareness is bound sooner or later to cease functioning altogether. To expect to maintain an attitude of love and respect without a foundation in deeper awareness would be like expecting a plant to flourish without proper soil.

As Emerson put it in his essay *The Over-Soul*: "I feel . . . that [something] higher in each of us overlooks this by-play, and Jove nods to Jove from behind each of us. *Men descend to meet.*"

Unless a couple view their marriage expansively, their union will not prove, in the fullest sense, successful. The very *basis* of true marriage is love reaching up to the heights.

❧ "Physician, Heal Thyself" ❧

Respect for one another should include giving each other the freedom to grow and to change, each at his own pace. Women who expect a second Jesus Christ for a husband would do better to enter a convent. And men who want perfection in their wives might as well marry a statue.

In India, men too often demand that their wives be like Sita, the devoted wife of Rama in the great epic poem, the *Ramayana*. Sita, to Indians, was the embodiment of wifely devotion and conjugal fidelity. To Indian husbands, then, I say, "If you want Sita for a wife, *you* be like Rama." For Rama himself never made demands of his wife. Rather, he tried to dissuade her from sacrificing herself for him.

A basic rule in life is to work with things as they *are*, not as we wish they were. This rule applies universally, and certainly no less so to relationships and to marriage. Accept your spouse as he or she *is*. Only by such acceptance will you have a chance of encouraging the potentials that exist for improvement.

Would you like to see your partner change? First, introspect; see whether the need isn't really for an inner change in yourself. So, maybe you'd like him to be like Jesus Christ: Are *you* the Virgin Mary? And so, maybe you'd like her to be like Sita: Are *you* Lord Rama? As a wise sage once put it, "Do you want to change the world? Change yourself!"

But it would be simplistic to claim that one is *always* at fault, when he sees flaws in others. The scriptural commandment not to judge others means not to *dislike* them for their flaws. It is not meant as a counsel to be unobservant. The test of whether your observation is judgmental is whether your own feelings are negatively affected, either by the person or by what is being done.

So then, what if you see flaws in your partner's character? The chances are that he, or she, being human, has a normal share of them. Ought you, then, to try to get your spouse to change?

If your effort is rooted in love, and if your concern is for *his* (or for *her*) happiness, not for your own, you have a duty to offer help. But that help must always be offered in the right way.

Discussing Differences

It is seldom wise to offer advice, as such. To offer it to one's spouse, particularly, can prove disastrous! Remember, you are not your partner's teacher. (How many couples try to assume that role to one another!) Even when he or she *asks* for your advice, treat the request with great sensitivity.

Never criticize. *Offer* your ideas—tentatively, as a friend—mentally leaving the other person entirely free to accept or reject them. No one *owes* it to you to take even your best advice. Tell yourself, rather, that the other person does *you* a favor, when accepting it.

Try never to speak under the influence of emotion. And never go deeply into a matter with your spouse if his or her emotions are upset. Strong emotions abhor reason.

Do plan to talk out your differences, however. No good will come from suppressing them. (It is amazing how often hurt feelings and misunderstandings, once one summons up the courage to confront them, simply evaporate.) But it isn't suppression if you put your suggestion mentally on a shelf until the right moment arrives to bring it out.

Speak when both of you are calm. And wait, if possible, for the time when what you have to say is likely to prove beneficial. Admittedly, waiting requires patience, but then, without patience no lasting good is ever accomplished. In counseling people, I myself have sometimes waited years for the right moment to say something that needed to be said all that time. Had I spoken sooner, it would have been like pulling an unripe fruit from a tree. Usually in these cases—not always—when I did speak, my words proved lastingly helpful.

A final point needs to be made on this subject. People sometimes suppress what they'd like to say, then tell themselves later, "Oh, it wasn't all that important," and never say it at all. Suppressed energy will find a release, eventually. If it can't be released charitably and in truth, it will find its expression in other ways that may prove considerably more harmful than simply talking it out *now*, with or without emotion. Whether to wait, then, before speaking depends on your ability to wait charitably.

❧ Giving Strength to One Another ❧

An important guideline for married couples is to strive always to give one another *strength*, and not to contribute to one another's weaknesses. This may sound obvious, but it is surprising how many couples reinforce each other's negativity. They agree with a dissatisfaction, for example, not always because they themselves are dissatisfied personally, but for the more dubious purpose of accumulating credits against such a time as they may want their own negativity reinforced.

One of the most insidious aspects of marriage, once one allows deliberate negativity to enter the relationship, is the tendency toward increasing, not decreasing, one another's delusions. In this manner, marriage, which ought to encourage mutual giving and assistance, can actually pose a formidable barrier to personal development.

Think in terms of the longer rhythms, not of the shorter ones. Keep your sense of over-all proportion. Remember, your commitment is to a lifelong relationship. Don't get swept up in the exigencies or the excitement of the moment.

It is easy to forget, during a momentary pique, how insignificant this feeling is compared to the over-all depth of your love for one another. Don't allow yourself, even by the tone of your voice, to convey, along with your displeasure, the much more shattering (and, one hopes, untrue) message, "I don't love you."

If it is your partner who is upset, *you* be the peacemaker. Never play games with your love. There is too much at stake. Why start a contest between you? If you can be the peacemaker this time, maybe your spouse will play the same role for you some other time, when *you* are upset.

Dignity, then, is an important concept also, crucial for growing together. Live calmly at your own center, that there be wisdom as well as love in all that you do together, and in all that you do for one another.

Finally, don't make situations, or things, or *anything* more important in your relationship than the love and respect you bear one another. For circumstances change. Compared to the long-term relationship you are building together, outer circumstances are fleeting. Your relationship, if you nurture it wisely and sensitively, may carry you past the portals of this life into eternity.

A sage was wont to give his disciples these simple words of advice: "Learn to behave." At first glance, this counsel may not seem particularly profound, but may remind one rather of that basically meaningless exhortation, "Be good." Yet these simple words are rich with practical counsel.

They speak, for one thing, to a common failing of mankind: the tendency to expect others to overlook our bad behavior so long as our *intentions* are good.

Don't fall into this mistake in your marriage. Let your behavior reflect your true and deeper feelings. Don't let carelessness and inattention inadvertently damage the beautiful work of art you are sculpting together.

❧ Points to Remember ❧

1. Never allow any decision to take precedence over your abiding commitment to each other.

2. A good motto in marriage is, *People are more important than things.*

3. Respect and consideration are the simple kindnesses in human relationships that, like oil, keep the machinery of life flowing smoothly.

4. To reject courtesy, when it is extended, is to invite its several alternatives. Marriage should be rooted in courtesy and respect.

5. Marriage, like life itself, ought to be an ever-expanding experience. To be such, it must be ever creative.

6. One suggestion for bringing creativity to your marriage is to do one thing every day to give special pleasure to your beloved.

7. Marriage is like flowing water: As long as it is given creative input, it will retain its freshness.

8. Perfect union cannot be achieved physically or mentally only: It must be sought above all in soul-union.

9. True growth in marriage is possible only if each partner assumes personal responsibility for their growth together.

10. Mutual respect flourishes best when a degree of distance, mutually agreed upon, is maintained.

11. Love is a giving and a sharing: It is not a taking.

12. Marriage is such a sensitive relationship that if in any way you try to coerce your partner, you risk damaging your relationship irretrievably.

13. Respect one another's free will. This respect should include giving each other the freedom to grow and change, each at his own pace.

14. A basic rule in life is to work with things as they *are*, not as we wish they were.

15. It is seldom wise to offer advice, as such.

16. Never criticize. *Offer*—tentatively, as a friend—mentally leaving the other person free to accept or reject your offering. No one owes it to you to take even your best advice.

17. Try never to speak under the influence of emotion. Speak when both of you are calm.

18. An important guideline for married couples is to strive always to give one another *strength*, and not to contribute to one another's weaknesses.

19. Think in terms of the longer rhythms.

20. If it is your partner who is upset, *you* be the peacemaker. Never play games with your love; there is too much at stake.

21. Live calmly at your own center, that there be wisdom as well as love in all that you do together, and in all that you do for one another.

Chapter Seven

Commitment

"Will you marry me?"

"Sure. Why not?" (A brief pause while she addresses the task of shifting a wad of chewing gum to the other side of her mouth.) "If it doesn't work, we can always get divorced."

This casual attitude toward what ought to be a sacred commitment has become prevalent nowadays. The statistics on divorce are alarming. Much has been said on the subject of the suffering it causes the children of a broken marriage. That, of course, is a very real part of the problem. But the suffering it causes the divorced couple, whether parents or not, is great also. Beneath the casual pose of indifference, and beneath the more actual anger and recriminations, there is deep personal tragedy. No matter how indifferent the superficial attitude, there remains an underlying sense of guilt, of self-doubt, of sorrow in the realization that something so beautiful should have ended torn and misshapen—like a tree after a hurricane.

There is much grief to be borne in life. Not least among them is the grief connected with divorce. Often, those who seem the most blasé about it are the ones suffering the most, inwardly.

Yet when St. Paul said, "It is better to marry than to burn," he overlooked a natural corollary to his statement:

"It is better to divorce than to burn in the fires of marital disharmony." Marriage that fails in its primary purpose of helping couples to grow together; marriage that is stagnant, or that keeps both partners bound in an earthly hell for the sake of a barren commitment: such marriages, surely, are not unions at all. They are simply shared incarceration.

People sometimes remain together not because they love each other, and not because there is any hope of their growing in unison toward any ideal at all, but only because of what other people might say. Their marriage is deadly to both partners, for it kills their enthusiasm, their interest in life, their very intelligence. They become walking corpses, waiting only for the undertaker to accept what they have been offering him mentally for years.

Such couples sometimes remain together not only for fear of losing face, but because they feel they are obeying some higher principle. But a principle has been misunderstood, surely, if it bears no fruit. Scriptural declarations against marriage, too, must be weighed in the scale of their fundamental purpose. As Jesus Christ put it, "The Sabbath was made for man, not man for the Sabbath."

No one will fault a couple's loyalty and steadfastness for staying together through thick and thin. True principles, however, like truth itself, are forever alive, not brittle and lifeless. Truth, like every living thing, must be adaptable to circumstances if it is to survive the tempests of earthly existence.

The purpose of marriage is mutual growth and expansion. To cling to a marriage solely because one feels one must is to defeat that very purpose. It amounts, usually, to covering under a blanket of artificial flowers the naked but actual reason for remaining in a dead relationship: pride. Such people cannot acknowledge that they have made a mistake, and cannot allow others to perceive them as having erred.

Commitment is a fundamental principle in every relationship. The failure of a commitment causes pain to everyone concerned. It is important, therefore, to understand what commitment means. It is important to learn how to commit oneself in the right way, to the right ends, and to the right person.

❦ What Is Commitment? ❧

Marriage is, or should be, a lifelong commitment. This means it should be undertaken with lifelong goals in mind. The more closely one's commitment can be allied to abiding principles, and not merely to a person, the more certain it will be to endure. For people may change, but principles are eternal.

The rose is beautiful. We enjoy its color, its shape, its fragrance. Should our enjoyment in the rose become excessive, however, our enjoyment will inevitably lead to disappointment. For the rose soon dies.

I once read an "Ann Landers" column in the newspaper in which some man expressed his "disillusionment" with his wife because she had put on weight. Ann Landers quite rightly called him a fool.

Because our lives are much longer than that of a rose, we see many roses come and go during the course of our lifetime. Thus, the loss of a prized rose doesn't make us bitter or cynical about floral beauty ("Well, all right, so roses are beautiful, but what good is beauty if it doesn't last?"); we soon understand that beauty is not a thing, but an abstraction. Things die, but the abstractions they represented remain untouched by death.

To marry a person for his or her beauty is like binding oneself to a cloud. Disappointment over the ending of a sunset is minimal, for a sunset is too brief for people to develop attachment to it. Bodily beauty lasts longer than an evening, but once it passes it, too, proves not much different from the ending of a beautiful sunset—except for our attachment to it. That which once was shining is gone. The pain in the loss is minimal, if our love was not so much for the shining cloud as for the eternal principle of beauty.

In every commitment, we should seek that, especially, which never changes. People's outward appearance changes, obviously. So also do their personalities, their interests, their tastes, opinions, and ideas. If your commitment is to any of these, it is likely to prove fragile. Commit yourself, therefore, to that which lasts.

Some people commit themselves to marriage as a principle. This is a wholesome view of matrimony; it enables couples to survive many trials together.

Other people feel a bond with one another on a soul level. This deeper commitment enables them to weather many storms.

The Indian scriptures counsel couples to love God in each other. This attitude may account for the exceptionally high number of happy marriages in India.

In every case, what we see is that the more one's commitment is to a principle, and offered to a specific individual in the name of that principle, the more that commitment will be likely to endure—and not to endure, merely, but to flourish and become ever-increasingly a source of happiness, growth, and mutual harmony.

Modern people, schooled to concentrate on the particular—"*this* car, *this* house, *this* painting, *this* person"—easily become disillusioned, to be swept on from one attachment to another. An Indian friend of mine once said to me, "You Americans pride yourselves on your lack of superstition. Well, frankly, I can't imagine a greater superstition than this one: your strange belief that happiness can be derived from mere *things*!"

To be excessively engrossed in the particular results either in excessive grief over its loss—which occurs inevitably, sooner or later—or in such a superficial commitment that one's loyalties shift with color change in the lighting. "I loved him so much when he had all his hair" is not vastly different from, "I loved him so much for his sense of humor, but now that he no longer laughs, I find I don't love him any more." And if these examples don't ring true to you, look for others that do. You will find them to be no less superficial.

Human nature is, of course, attracted by outer glamour. The roots of a plant may be more important to it than its leaves, but who will pretend that on that account the roots are as attractive? In marriage, romantic affinity is the given. What I am saying is, marriage needs much more than romance to succeed.

The important thing is to understand that what you get with a spouse is the whole plant. The more wedded in thought you are to attractions that are merely outward, the more fickle your affections will be.

◈ Worshiping Likes and Dislikes ◈

If there is one obstacle to self-development greater even than suppression, it is fickleness. Suppression is a stoked fire: It can cause harm when it breaks out, as it must, eventually, but if it is channeled wisely it can provide great powers of accomplishment. Fickleness, on the other hand, merely scatters energy. Fickle people rarely, if ever, accomplish anything worthwhile in their lives.

Fickleness comes from concentrating too much on outer glamour, and too little on real worth.

One of the delusions of our times is the emphasis placed on "feeling good" about things. Many people confuse intuitive feeling with mere likes and dislikes. In marriage, they may get divorced merely because they no longer "feel good" about being together.

I've stressed the need for developing intuition. It is important to add that, just as there are different levels of commitment, so also there are different levels of intuition. Many feelings, moreover, that make a show of being intuitive are not really so at all.

As some people allow themselves to be guided in their commitments by how they *feel* today (as opposed to how they felt yesterday), so also there are people who justify every feeling by calling it intuitive. Before long, a kind of tornado develops: "I don't feel as loving toward you today as I did yesterday; my 'intuition' tells me there's something wrong in our relationship; that makes me *feel* badly; my intuition tells me our marriage is on a downward spiral: Perhaps it was all a mistake. Perhaps we never should have gotten married in the first place. Perhaps we should file for a divorce." Emotional feelings feed a shallow intuition of what is actually no more than a fleeting misunderstanding, thus stirring mere mood-swings in interpersonal relationships into mighty whirlpools.

At such times, it is better to ignore feeling altogether, and apply the discipline of common sense. Indeed, basic to every marriage should be a commitment, not to feeling, but to truth—to what is *right*.

❧ Thinking of Others ❧

Responsibility in marriage seems almost passé nowadays. It had better be brought back, for without a sense of responsibility there can be few lasting unions. It is more important to be dutiful than to worry at every turn over how one "feels" about things.

Women, as I said earlier, tend to be more intuitive than men because they are more aware on a level of feeling. Men, relying more on logic, may lose touch with their feelings. If they do so, they sacrifice the native gift of intuition. The advantage men have in developing intuition is that the intellect, once it relinquishes an exaggerated attachment to logic, has a calming influence on the emotions, thereby producing that calm feeling which is intuition.

Intuitive feeling must not be confused with personal likes and dislikes. Often people will say, "I *feel* that is a good direction to go," when what they really mean is, "I *want* to go that way," or, "I *like* that direction." Calm, intuitive feeling has nothing to do with such emotional "guidance." That is why our feelings need the direction of reason and common sense. The intellect, on the other hand, must not rely on logic alone for understanding, lest, like a bloodhound deprived of its sense of smell, it go baying down innumerable false trails. When reason draws its inspiration from calm feeling, and when calm feeling is kept in a state of reason, only then may the result be called intuition.

The calmer the feeling, the deeper the intuition. The deeper (because calmer) the intuitive understanding of a relationship, the more enduring one's commitment to it will be.

To commit yourself to the right ends in marriage is to desire a relationship that will be of value not only to you and your spouse, but also to other people. Only such a relationship is truly expansive. Any marriage that focuses entirely on the relationship of two people to each other proves cloying at last. Life, to be truly fulfilling, should be a service to all.

Couples should tell each other on the very day of their wedding, "I want to make you happy." Finding happiness in each other, they should turn outward to others with the thought: "Let us make everyone happy!"

The right ends in marriage imply no finish line, but a directional movement of ever greater expansion; a service of love to others that, ultimately, embraces the whole world as one's larger family.

If your commitment is to a principle, and to your marriage partner as someone with whom you plan to develop in that principle, then if your partner later rejects the principle, and no amount of patience on your part shows evidence of effecting a change, the best for you both may be to separate.

If separate you must, do so with dignity. Better that than to get drawn downward into decreasing attunement with that principle, through bickering and misunderstandings. If you must separate, part with respect, and with love.

First, however, do your very best to make it work. Try to help your spouse, even if you do not see that you yourself are being helped. For in giving we often gain more than we realize. Marriage is an important commitment, and ought not to be abandoned until every other avenue has been tried.

The importance of choosing the right marriage partner becomes obvious from looking at the number of marriages that end in failure. To choose the right marriage partner, seek someone, above all, who shares your ideals. For if you yourself are unselfish, but your wife or husband cannot escape the vortex of self-involvement, marriage between you is likely to prove barren.

❧ Points to Remember ❧

1. To marry a person for his, or for her, beauty is like binding yourself to a cloud. In every commitment, seek that, especially, which never changes.

2. The more one's commitment is to a principle, and offered to another person in the name of that principle, the more that commitment is likely to endure.

3. To be engrossed in the particular results in grief over its loss.

4. If there is one obstacle to self-development greater even than suppression, it is fickleness.

5. One of the delusions of our times is the emphasis placed on "feeling good" about things. Many people confuse intuitive feeling with mere likes and dislikes.

6. Basic to every marriage should be a commitment, not to feeling, but to truth—to what is right.

7. The calmer the feeling, the deeper the intuition. The deeper (because calmer) the intuitive understanding of a relationship, the more enduring one's commitment to it will be.

8. To commit yourself to the right ends in marriage means to desire a relationship that will help not only yourselves, but other people.

9. Couples should tell each other on their wedding day, "I want to make you happy."

10. The right ends in marriage imply no finish line, but a directional movement toward ever greater expansion.

11. If separate you must, after all else has been tried, do so with dignity. Do so with respect, and with love.

12. To choose the right marriage partner, look for someone above all who shares your ideals.

Chapter  *Eight*

Sex in Marriage

A marriage is generally considered to be consummated when it has resulted in sexual union. This is, of course, a definition born of society's concern for its own continuity. That concern, however, also leads to a definition of marriage itself as an institution devoted primarily to sexual union. Yet even in sexual union there is so much more than "having sex." What about sex as a way of expressing love? What about sex as a means of deepening a couple's feelings of love and tenderness for each other? What about defining their relationship in terms of these feelings, rather than in terms of physical passion?

Yes, of course marriage enables couples to perpetuate the species. In addition, as St. Paul rather crudely put it, "It is better to marry than to burn." Marriage enables people to create a union for which their physical nature demands an outlet. On a more positive note, marriage also promotes a deeper union than can be achieved through promiscuity.

At the same time, we are more than animals, and ought to view marriage itself, and the physical aspects of marriage, as a road to consummation of a higher kind.

In the highest sense, consummation in marriage should be considered only to *include* sexual union, while promising that sort of union which bestows a subtler-than-physical fulfillment.

This point is important where the sexual aspects of marriage are considered. For, from a social standpoint, mores limiting human sexuality are directed primarily at creating a stable environment for the raising of children. Society is not concerned with the spiritual overtones of marriage, nor with sexual abstinence within marriage. Married couples are encouraged, rather, to enjoy sexual intercourse as often as possible. It is considered the prize they have earned for accepting the social responsibility of matrimony.

Until the sexual aspects of marriage are brought under control, however, and made a consummation of love rather than of passion, the higher goals of marriage will remain elusive.

☙ The Higher Purpose of Sex ❧

Sexual union fulfills two purposes: It is, of course, necessary for the propagation of the species. It is also important as an affirmation of selfless love. In the first case, there is no viable alternative; all couples who desire children must engage in sexual union. But as an affirmation of love, sex ought not to be limited to the physical act of coition. Coition should be considered only a stage in the development of deeper marital ties. Couples who never grow beyond the physical stage are unlikely ever to plumb the depths of true love.

For it is difficult, in sexual intercourse, to exclude the element of self-indulgence—that is to say, of selfishness. True love is self-giving.

Non-physical love between the sexes is often spoken of as "Platonic" love. Actually, Plato's ideal was that couples would come together sexually in the beginning, and then gradually over the years refine their love so that to affirm it sexually became diminishingly important. Platonic love does not, strictly speaking, mean soul-love as *opposed to* sexual love. It means, rather, a natural shift of emphasis *from* the physical *to* the spiritual.

Physical affection is a natural part of being human. It can be made beautiful. It can also be made selfish and demanding, and therefore not affection at all, but a mere and ugly pretense. Humankind has the potential to grow beyond animal passion and desire. If a person aspires toward that potential, he must view not only marriage but *every* relationship in terms of higher fulfillments.

To mix with others for what you can get out of them is to be selfish, not sharing. Passion is selfish; it is not, in itself, a giving act. Greed is selfish. Desire directed toward personal gratification is, essentially, selfish. To mix with others not in a spirit of selfish desire, but in joy, is self-liberating. Relationships that are based on sharing are endlessly rewarding. But relationships that are rooted in mutual need result in a downward spiral of inter-dependency.

If these principles hold true in other relationships, it is only natural that they should hold true in marriage. As a couple grow closer together, it is important for them to build a relationship in which passion and desire are transformed into self-giving love.

Such, alas, is the power of social conditioning that what is perfectly natural becomes judged as unnatural. Let us face it, we live in an age that places every possible emphasis on sex. One sees hardly an advertisement for such essentially asexual objects as cigarettes, automobiles, or candy that doesn't in some way suggest to the prospective buyer that purchasing them will subtly increase his sexual prowess or fulfillment.

❧ The Credo of Pleasure ❧

One might even say of these "enlightened" times that we have abandoned medieval theology only to formulate an insidious modern theology of our own: a *credo* of pleasure, which views sex as life's greatest imaginable fulfillment. And if you are married and can still enjoy sexual union at the age of ninety-five or a hundred—why, glorious! wonderful! Pity those poor dotards, indeed, who don't feel impelled to enjoy it every day.

Truth, however, has a way of finding its way out into the light, no matter how carefully it has been hidden in the basement. The other day a friend of mine overheard two people speaking of the commonest causes of divorce. "If it isn't religion," one remarked, "it's sex!"

The plain truth is, *no* sense pleasure can continue to be enjoyable, if it is over-indulged. Stated more positively, *all* sense pleasures are enhanced by moderation. This is as true of eating, partying, and good music as it is of sex. With excessive indulgence, what may have begun as enjoyment inevitably declines into mere habit.

With sexual union, moreover, other important factors must be considered. One of these is the fact that there are *two* people's feelings involved. One person's definition of moderation may be another's definition of over-indulgence. If partners fail to take each other's feelings into account, the sex act becomes what it inclines all too easily to be in any case: an act of self-gratification, not of love; of taking, not of giving; of mere supply and demand, not of sensitive and mutual sharing.

Between "having sex" and "making love" there is a world of difference. The latter may or may even not include sexual union. The real purpose behind making love is to express tenderness; the act should not be made an end in itself. If it takes time and effort to develop the ability to "make love" sensitively, the rewards are worth the cost. For the sex act to be truly loving, then, it must be rooted in self-control.

Moderation in sex is important for another reason also. Unlike other sense pleasures, such as the enjoyment of good music, the sex act represents an expenditure, not an absorption or an increase, of energy.

This is not to say that to expend energy need necessarily be enervating; often, indeed, we draw more energy to ourselves by *using* what we already have. The opposite is true also: By continued disuse we may find we have less energy to draw on when we need it—even as a stream grows stagnant when its water ceases to flow. Thus, after expending energy in a healthful hike or run, you may feel yourself glowing with vitality; whereas, if you spent the same amount of time home in bed in the hope of thereby conserving your strength, you might be actually enervated by your idleness.

❧ The Flow of Energy in the Body ❧

To understand how the sex act relates to the flow of energy, it is important, first, to understand how it is that energy can be awakened in the body—indeed, drawn to it at will. For physical energy is not produced only by the food we eat.

Haven't you ever performed a task willingly and actually felt *more* energy than when you started? How does that compare with times when you performed similar tasks reluctantly? On these occasions, the work tired you, didn't it?

Life-affirming attitudes of joy, willingness, or love actually *generate* energy in the body. And life-negating attitudes of sadness, unwillingness, or animosity actually sap the body's energy.

These are simple truths, and easily tested. More is involved than getting enough to eat. How, then, to explain them?

Bear in mind, first, that dictum of modern science that matter is really a vibration of energy. Our physical bodies are vibrations of energy. The material universe is an ocean of *energy*. In the body, energy provides the link between body and mind. By will we send energy to the body—to make an arm move, for instance. By positive will power, also, we can draw on the energy in the universe around us. By negative will power—for example, by fear or discouragement, we close ourselves off from that energy source.

Surrounded as we are by energy, and living in bodies that are, essentially, vibrations of energy, there is nothing to stop us from partaking of that energy—nothing, that is to say, but our lack of awareness of it. In any case, we draw on that energy-source, to a greater or lesser degree, all the time.

I myself practice a system of "energization" exercises that was developed by my spiritual teacher, Paramhansa Yogananda. By means of these exercises one can draw consciously on the cosmic source of energy, at will. I have practiced this system daily for years, and can attest that it accomplishes wonders. Among its other benefits, it produces a constant inner flow of vitality and well-being.

The axiom on which these exercises are based, and a good motto on which to build our lives, is, "The greater the will, the greater the flow of energy." Yogananda taught that by the strong exertion of will power coupled with a sensitive awareness of the body's energy, one can tap into the infinite energy-source, and keep the body and brain invigorated all the time.

This book is hardly the place for expounding this teaching in detail, but I hope that what I have written here will find support from your own experience. Attitudes of willingness, joy, and love, in short, are not merely the *result* of a healthy abundance of energy in the body: They actually *create* this abundance, and increase it.

As Dale Carnegie put it in his famous dictum: "Act enthusiastic, and you'll *be* enthusiastic!"

When couples come together lovingly and joyfully in physical union, they naturally experience an increase of energy resulting from their union. From whence stems this increase? From the sex act itself? Is it not, rather, quite separately produced by their love and joy?

Look at those couples for whom sex has ceased to be a joy, and has become a mere habit. How often such people seem utterly bored with life, and with one another; moody and irritable; prematurely old; increasingly un-self-fulfilled.

It may be argued, in these cases, that sex is not the culprit. It can be definitely stated, however, that nor has it proved the *cure* for their boredom and lack of energy. In fact, it is joy and love, not sexual union, that are the true causes of any increase of energy that people derive from sexual union.

To state this truth more simply, *no merely mechanical act that expends energy can by itself replenish it*. The runner who jogs dispiritedly will return home exhausted; it is the joyful jogger who returns refreshed. In the sex act, similarly, the mere mechanics of sex cannot possibly increase one's supply of energy; they can only, to some extent at least, deplete it.

For men, especially, the body must work hard to produce semen—that highly refined essence which represents the very cream of the body's productivity. When this inner activity becomes strained by excessive sexuality, the cream is diluted. The body itself, moreover, must then direct more energy toward the production of semen—and thereby deflect energy away from other important inner functions.

The consequences may not be observable at once, nor in clear (because immediate) relation to sexual activity itself; years spent in such activity, however, will result in a greater susceptibility to ill health; in nervousness, depression, loss of inner harmony, a decrease of mental clarity, and general lack of vitality.

The youth who fondly believes that he can indulge in sex nightly discovers only years later the more serious symptoms of his self-abuse. By then he may blame them on a host of outward misfortunes. He may even seek illusory escape in ever more strenuous sexuality—like a fish that seeks to escape the fisherman's net by burrowing deeper into the mud instead of leaping over the side of the net to safety in the sea.

Young men, then, who think by constant indulgence to "prove" their masculinity, would do better to try to prove it in ways that will *reinforce* it, not waste it. Such ways would include developing their determination and will power, and their ability to reason clearly. For such development, self-control is a definite aid.

Women, too, suffer an energy-loss from sexual over-indulgence, though much less so than men. In their lives, also, the effects—similar to those in the case of men—become evident only after the passing of years.

A cosmetic company once did a survey to find out who, among various groups of women, had the best complexions. The results were not anything the company could use in its advertising campaign: The single group of women with the best complexions were nuns!

The energy gain that people experience from sexual union is due to the consciousness they hold during the act—to their love, and their joy—and not to the act itself. Furthermore, this love and joy cannot but diminish, the more the sex act is allowed to sink to the level of habit. To approach a thing joyfully, it is necessary to treat it as something special, and not "have at it" merely because it is night again, and you're in bed, and—well, *there* she is.

❧ The Way of Moderation ❧

Everything in life becomes less precious—even stale—the more it is used. You may love beautiful music, but if you listen to it constantly it will eventually annoy you. Flowers are delightful, but a plethora of them can easily become tiresome.

The Japanese make a practice of putting only one lovely object on display in the home at a time. A wise custom. An even wiser lesson.

I have said that it is by their love and joy that people find an increase of energy in the sex act. Well, then—love and joyful sharing aside—wouldn't enthusiasm for the act itself, according to the principles I have outlined, draw more energy into the body also, even if it was motivated entirely by the desire for self-gratification?

Yes, in fact, it would, and to some extent it does. But an important distinction needs to be made here. For the grosser or more animalistic the thought, the grosser also the manifestation of energy. Energy that is directed only toward sexual gratification manifests literally on a lower plane—that is to say, in a lower vortex in the spine—lower, for instance, than love, whose vortex is in the region of the heart.

Have you ever noticed how, when you feel uplifted, your energy and consciousness seem literally to flow upward? Even your eyes tend to gaze upward. It is no accident that we use words like "uplifted," "high," "elated," and expressions like

"I feel on top of the world!" to describe our mood when we are spiritually at our best. Nor is it an accident that we say we feel "low," "depressed," "downcast," or "in the dumps" when we feel spiritually out of tune.

Energy that is limited in its manifestation to the base of the spine generates in the mind thoughts of selfishness, cynicism, and all the other sad children of a wholly materialistic outlook on life. Thus, while selfless love ennobles the mind, sex for mere self-gratification eventually debases it, developing in one a coarse nature, and blinding one to finer perceptions.

Let your physical union, then, be an expression of love. To keep it that way, let it be only occasional; that is to say, let it be an *occasion.*

The way of moderation may be described as the way of nature. This point is made in a profound little book by Yogananda's guru, Sri Yukteswar, *The Holy Science.* As this book states, the sexual impulse has both a natural and a diseased state.

In the diseased state, sexual desire, like a fever, draws excessive energy to itself and demands constant gratification. In the natural state, however, the sexual craving seeks only infrequent outlet.

The major cause of the diseased state, Sri Yukteswar explained, is an unnatural diet: The toxins produced thereby settle in the lower intestines and irritate the sex nerves.*

---

* In his book—and also in my own home study course, *Fourteen Steps to Higher Awareness* [later retitled *The Art and Science of Raja Yoga* —ed.]—the reader will find information on the most natural diet for man.

⚜ The Influence of Upbringing ⚜

There are other causes, besides diet, for unnatural sexual excitation. These were not mentioned in *The Holy Science*, perhaps because the author, writing in the 1890s, did not have to deal with a society as sexually stimulated as our own. Nowadays, because society as a whole is afflicted by the disease of excess, it is difficult even for people who otherwise eat and live properly to avoid the contagion.

Modern upbringing is the culprit. For what influence is likely to reach children from an adult world in which hardly a billboard, book cover, movie, or television advertisement misses the opportunity to convey in some way the message: "Sex is the *answer!*"?

The greatest hope for the future is right education. Children need to be taught to use the creative impulse wisely. Those who do so will find it easier later, as adults, to base their marriages on mature principles.

For now, however, most adults will need to proceed gradually, naturally, and with common sense in their efforts to achieve sublimation. Extreme efforts at self-control may, indeed, create more problems than they solve.

I advise "making haste slowly" because I have met many couples who, having read that sexual self-control is an ideal, develop serious inner conflicts about their relationship together. They may indulge in the sex act in response to a physical need, but afterward they feel guilty for having done so. The husband may end up seeing his wife as a temptress. The wife may start wondering if she made a mistake in ever marrying in the first place.

❧ Spiritualizing Sex ❧

It is important to understand that one does not escape physical attachments by calling them ugly. One escapes bondage to sex by spiritualizing and beautifying it—by making it more a communion of heart and soul than of two bodies; by realizing that sex is not only coition: It is a loving touch, a smile, a gentle embrace, a shared warmth that may require no other expression to be fully satisfying.

Sex, finally, can be spiritualized by learning to see God in the act, then, gradually, concentrating more and more on pure love. In other words, there should be an inward consciousness of joy, of communion with the Divine, and with the Divine in one another—of participation in His infinite love even while making love physically.

In this way, by gradual, natural degrees, people find that they don't really need that outward affirmation of love for love to shine in their hearts just as strongly. Indeed, this kind of love is the deepest, purest marital love of all.

This point of inner freedom will never be achieved, however, if sex becomes something to hate, something to feel guilty about and suppress.

What, then, about another alternative altogether—renunciation? *Ought* one to marry?

It isn't possible to make a general rule. For some people, certainly, renunciation is the straightest and safest route to soul-freedom. But I have seen people who wanted, at first, to live a celibate life, but who later married, finding that it was only *after* marriage that they achieved spiritual stability in their lives.

Always it will depend on the individual, on his or her personal needs. In true moral law there are no absolutes, only directions. On the path of inner growth, particularly, every effort should be made to take people where they *are*, not where some abstract rule or dogma says they ought to be, and to develop them by natural degrees—always with common sense—in the direction of their own ultimate fulfillment.

Once people understand the direction that marriage should take, they can use every aspect of marriage to help them to grow spiritually. As long as they retain a strong physical consciousness in marriage, there will probably be far more of the upsets, the hurts, the false expectations, and the demands that are, all too often, the bane of matrimony.

Once you and your spouse expand your relationship to a level of truly selfless love, you will find a real increase in your affection for each other. As you perfect the love between you, you will find entering into your marriage a kind of sweetness, a mutual respect and communion that will be, for both of you, a source of perennial joy.

❧ Points to Remember ❧

1. In the highest sense, consummation in marriage should be considered only to include sexual union, while promising that sort of union which bestows subtler-than-physical fulfillment.

2. Until the sexual aspects of marriage are brought under control, and made a consummation of love rather than of passion, the higher goals of marriage must remain elusive.

3. Physical affection is a natural part of being human. It can be made beautiful. It can also be made selfish and demanding, in which case it is not affection at all, but a mere pretense.

4. No sense pleasure can continue to be enjoyable, if it is over-indulged. Stated more positively, *all* sense pleasures are enhanced by moderation.

5. Between "having sex" and "making love" there is a world of difference. The real purpose behind making love is to express tenderness; the act should not be made an end in itself.

6. The youth who fondly believes that he can indulge in sex with impunity discovers only years later the more serious symptoms of his self-abuse.

7. Young men, then, who think by constant indulgence to "prove" their masculinity, would do better to try to prove it in ways that will *reinforce* it, not waste it.

8. Let your physical union be an expression of love. To keep it that way, let it be only occasional; that is to say, let it be an *occasion*.

9. The greatest hope for the future is right education. Children need to be taught to use the creative impulse wisely.

10. One does not escape physical attachments by calling them ugly. One escapes bondage to sex by spiritualizing and beautifying it—by making it more a communion of heart and soul than of two bodies.

11. As you perfect the love between you, you will find entering your marriage a kind of sweetness, a mutual respect and communion that will be, for both of you, a source of perennial joy.

Chapter Nine

Communication

The strains felt in marriage are often due to simple miscommunication. Men and women, often without being aware of the fact, tend to communicate in different ways.

The following conversational exchange is not necessarily typical, but it illustrates this tendency. In real life, the wife might express her wishes quite openly. Her tendency in many similar situations, nevertheless, will be to be indirect, especially if her feelings are refined. For whereas strong emotions may be, and often are, blurted out, calmer ones usually require a degree of delicacy for their expression.

Let us imagine a woman who wants to go out for the evening, but is uncertain of her husband's response. She may lead up to her proposal with seeming irrelevance. "Bob and Betty," she announces, referring to a couple they know, "go to the movies every week."

Men are more literal-minded, for literalness is a mark of logical thinking. It is not so much that men are immune to the delicate approach; more likely, they are simply blind to it. Thus, the woman's husband may miss the point altogether. If he takes the trouble to reply to what strikes him as an unfathomable comment, he may do so absent-mindedly, murmuring, "That's nice, dear." At this point his wife, if she goes by the rule book, will astound him by crying, "Oh, you never take me anywhere!"

Her husband gazes at her in astonishment. What a perfect non sequitur! Are all women, he asks himself, so utterly unreasonable?

Men are literal-minded—perhaps too much so. If a husband wants to go out, the chances are he will simply say so, and wait for his wife's comments on the subject. It won't occur to him that his wife might infer from his simple declaration that he is trying to impose his will on her.

"Why didn't he *ask* me?" she will demand later of her women friends, using this episode to justify her complaint that she finds her marriage oppressive. Meanwhile, she will probably say nothing to her husband, instead taking the "hurt" deeply inside, where she will let it fester until, weeks or months later, it breaks out on the slightest excuse, generally over some issue quite unrelated to the actual cause of misunderstanding.

When at last the husband is confronted with this episode and condemned for his "insensitivity," he stares at her in amazement. "Well," he demands, "why didn't you just *say* what you wanted? I'd have gone along with your wishes happily!"

The wife is usually more delicate in expressing her feelings. She finds it easier to express a desire by indirection. *How else* could she have taken his blunt declaration, except as an expression of intent that denied her own interests altogether?

And the husband, having expressed his interest, is perfectly willing to entertain any views she may have on the subject, whether pro or con. *How else* could he have opened the conversation, except by stating clearly—not aggressively—his inclination, thereby inviting a rational discussion of possible alternatives?

Husbands, once they achieve the status of Veterans of Marital Communication (VMC is, I believe, the official des-

ignation), will, of course, have learned to phrase their opening statement more carefully. Perhaps they will say, "There's a
good movie in town. Are you interested?" The trick seems to
be to address the wife's feelings without intruding your own,
realizing that she may assume that there are strong feelings
on your part even when you have none.

Rarely, indeed, do husbands oppose their wives' feelings
on a feeling level, unless they are the bullying type of male,
in which case they are usually lost to the refinements of both
feeling and reason. The normal husband, if he offers opposi-
tion, does so more often with the weapons of reason.

Both sexes must be careful not to use their special faculties oppressively. Women must not resort to emotional black-
mail. (Men who try that tactic usually succeed only in ap-
pearing childish.) And men must not use logic relentlessly to
force a reluctant agreement. Logic should be used to arrive
at the truth of a situation. Anyone, male or female, who em-
ploys it merely to score a victory is acting under the influence
of emotion, not of impersonal reason.

Cultural differences often create misunderstandings, also.
I remember once, at a party years ago, offering an Italian lady
a plate of tea sandwiches. "No, thank you," she said.

I, quite naturally (from my point of view), took the plate
on to the next person. At that point I heard her whisper to a
friend, "Why did he pass me by? I'm hungry!"

She had only wanted to be polite. According to her cultural conditioning, I should have repeated my offer, then
gently insisted.

Women are more apt to reject reason altogether, if their
feelings don't support a logical trend. Men, on the other
hand, are apt to reject feelings altogether *unless* they support
such a trend.

So you see, in communication between the sexes there is plenty of room for misunderstandings. Husbands and wives, both, may sometimes seek the company of their own sex simply in order to reaffirm their own sanity. Apart from the motivation of high ideals, it is easy for other reasons, also, to see why men and women enter monasteries, and difficult to understand why, in recent decades, so many monasteries have become emptied of votaries.

Well, to be serious: I think communication between the sexes is not only an art to be developed for the sake of harmony in the home. It is also important as a means of rounding out one's own character. Thus, the different ways in which men and women signal their thoughts and desires can make both of them more sensitive to complementary ways of thinking and feeling. Without this balance, each would have only a limited ability to understand himself.

❧ Bridging the Communication Chasm ❧

Here are a few pointers to help husbands and wives to develop better communication in their marriages:

1. Show appreciation, when you feel it.

Don't take your spouse's awareness of your appreciation for granted. Some people equate appreciation with flattery, or else feel that they are showing discernment by withholding praise until it is *really* merited. In the name of sincerity they unwittingly convey another impression altogether: indifference.

I have many friends in Germany. Occasionally, I've noticed, a few of them seem to feel that the best way to demonstrate their sincerity is to offer criticism. It is a cultural characteristic, but one that takes getting used to; people raised differently may see in this approach, not friendly concern, but veiled hostility.

The most important rule in communication is to put yourself in the other person's shoes. Don't ask yourself, "How can I best declare myself?" Ask, rather, "How will the other person best receive what I'd like to say?"

Appreciation is often a more important message than exactness of opinion. No one wants to feel, after all, that every day in the home is like sitting for an exam.

2. Never take your spouse's understanding for granted.

There is a human tendency, especially in close relationships, to assume too much understanding.

* Don't assume telepathic communication, even when you sometimes have it.

* Don't assume shared tastes. Rather, pay your spouse the compliment of not knowing his or her every wish in advance. (No one likes to be categorized.) When you show that you expect a certain response, make your expectation a sign of pleasure in the possession of this intimate knowledge, and not a yawning assumption that your spouse is utterly predictable.

* Don't assume the other person knows how you feel, simply because he or she *ought* to know. Otherwise, miscommunication gives way to non-communication.

* Assume *a desire* on your spouse's part for communication and understanding.

3. Listen to the other person at least as often as you want him to listen to you.

In marriage one sees a lot of silent partners. Observation tells me that this is very often a consequence of the silent one having been beaten verbally into non-communication. Don't be so exuberant in your desire to communicate that your speech is a hurricane, blowing all before it.

4. In any difference of opinion, don't insist on getting the last word.

Remember, in any difference of opinion, truth will be the final arbiter. Truth always wins in the end.

To give your spouse the last word—lovingly, not sarcastically—is itself a kind of victory.

5. Never play power games.

"Why don't you say something?"
Silence.
"Are you upset with me?"
(Nose in the air) "Not at all!"
"Come on, have I done something wrong?"
"*You* know what you've done."

This sort of game can go on indefinitely. Its sole purpose is to get the questioner on the defensive. Its rationale may be personal insecurity, but its *reality* is an attempt to gain power over, and to impose a sense of insecurity on, the other person.

Why? This game of power is demeaning to what ought to be the dignity of love.

Even if you feel slighted, maintain a noble attitude—not by endeavoring to show your partner how noble *you* are, but by showing complete acceptance and respect.

There is no need for you to react to the way others treat you. Live at your own divine center, and bow in silent respect to that center in others—especially in your own wife or husband.

6. Avoid, if possible, voicing negative emotions.

Paramhansa Yogananda used to say, "The mouth is the cannon, and the words that pass through it are the cannon balls. Many a prized friendship has been destroyed by a few thoughtless words."

It is rare for a person, under the influence of emotion, to state clearly what he really means, even if his speech, in the heat of the moment, is eloquent. For even if the words are well chosen, the eyes, the facial expressions, the gestures—all tell another story. And even if these are carefully disciplined to express calmness, the tone of voice still plays the traitor.

If you give vent, through ill-considered speech, to your emotions, you will regret your words later on. Or, even if you rejoice in them and feel that they "served him (or her) right," you will rue the episode later, when you discover what it has done to your relationship.

In the novel, *Love Story*, there is the famous definition of love: "Love is never having to say you're sorry." The beauty of this saying is that it implies a relationship in which respect and consideration are always held up as ideals. In real love, of course, there are plenty of times when one feels a need to say, "I'm sorry." For love is a growing process; it doesn't arrive on the threshold of marriage full-blown and perfect.

There is even a certain beauty and tenderness in the reconciliation sought by telling the other person, "I'm sorry." A jacket soon wears thin, however, if it is worn too frequently. Comport yourself in such a way that, as much as possible, you avoid having to apologize later.

Whenever you feel upset, pause a while. If possible, wait for calmness to return to its throne. Let calmness, not emotion, rule, and you will always be the emperor of your inner kingdom.

In calmness above all you will convey your *real* message, underlying your momentary upset. Then, even if you have a grievance to air, your partner, if he or she is sensitive, will get the additional message: "I really love you."

7. Learn to enjoy silence together.

Make your silences communicative, and not mere lapses in the conversation. Learn to reach out to your partner with psychic fingers, as it were. Love attains perfection in perfect stillness.

8. Pay attention to the tones of your voice.

Have you ever noticed how instantly your vocal tones reflect your psychological or emotional states? Jesus Christ said, "Out of the fullness of the heart the mouth speaketh." I've often wondered whether his reference wasn't to the very tones of a person's speech.

For the slightest mood shift betrays itself instantly. Irritation creates a tightening of the vocal cords. Love relaxes them. Tenderness, good humor, pride, enthusiasm, amusement, weakness, strength—all these and many more are reflected instantly in an alteration in the tones of your voice. If you haven't noticed these nuances, listen carefully the next time you or someone else speaks. By simply changing your tone of voice, you can actually improve a negative attitude.

I've often thought that singing teachers leave the greater body of true teaching on this subject unspoken by telling their students to develop only the sounding board of their bodies. The body's usefulness in this respect is merely that it can produce a loud sound, thereby filling a concert hall. This ability is no longer really necessary, now that superbly crafted microphones and loudspeaker systems reproduce the human voice so well. The difficulty with operatic technique is that it is difficult to shout, even melodiously, and at the same time express the subtle nuances of thought and feeling.

In a concert hall, it isn't always easy to tell, without a program before you, whether the famous opera singer is letting loose with a love ballad or summoning the troops to arms with a marching song. It is necessary to bellow in either case, simply to be heard in the back row. (And pity the poor heroine upon whose ear the tenor must inflict his love ballads, shattering the peace.)

There is a subtler "sounding board" than the physical body. It consists of certain centers of energy within the body. Love, for example, emanates from the spinal region just behind the heart. Concentrate there, and you will find that you can give greater vocal expression to the love you feel.

Calmness emanates from the cervical region just behind the throat.

Will power and joy emanate from the forehead, between the eyebrows. That is why people frown when expressing will power, or raise their eyebrows when feeling joy.

Try focusing the energy of your voice in the region of the heart. Then lift the sound up through the cervical region to the brain, and thence out through the forehead.

I wish I could go into this teaching more deeply here. The only way really to teach it, however, would be in person. On the other hand, people may also understand something of it by listening to recordings of my voice, which reflects, perhaps, my lifelong study of this subject.

To conclude, remember, the way you say a thing is every bit as important as *what* you say.

9. Learn to speak more with the eyes.

A reporter from the *Washington Post* interviewed me recently. I found it disconcerting not to be able to engage him in eye contact.

Nobody likes to converse with a talking mask. The eyes are well described as the windows of the soul. But people who don't *think with* their eyes while speaking—often for no other reason than the fact that they wear glasses, and are accustomed to hiding behind them—deprive themselves of half of their natural apparatus for communication.

Make the expression in your eyes part of the language you use for communication. Send energy through them—that energy which you are trying to express. Tell your eyes to participate in whatever positive feelings you entertain.

10. Hold realistic expectations of one another.

Don't expect perfection of your partner. Imperfection is, after all, inherent in the human race. Accept your partner as he or she is, not as you would like him (or her) to be. Only by recognizing and accepting reality as it is have we a hope of inspiring people to change for the better.

11. Make courtesy a normal part of your self-expression.

People too often think of courtesy as "company manners." Not at all. True courtesy is simply a mark of considerateness. It is the expression of a dignified nature, calmly centered in itself. Courtesy is a mark of respect, and respect is an important aspect of love.

12. Be slow to judge, but ever quick to forgive.

Very often there is a perfectly good explanation for what has been said or done. Try to give your partner the benefit of the doubt.

On the other hand, are *your* hands "squeaky clean"? "Blessed are the merciful," Jesus said, "for they shall obtain mercy."

If ever you feel wronged, and react in anger only to learn that your assessment of the situation was mistaken, admit your mistake readily. Don't *ever* allow yourself to remain committed to an error.

Again, when your partner tries to make amends, do your best to be gracious. To continue wielding your anger like a club, or enclosing yourself in dudgeon like a cloak, is to betray an attachment to anger that falls far short of your wedding commitment. It is an admission, rather, that you've been playing a marital power game, and that you've suffered a setback in it. Recognize what you are doing, give it a merry laugh inwardly, and relinquish the game.

ᣟ Points to Remember ᣟ

1. The strains felt in marriage are often due to simple mis-communication. Men and women, often without being aware of the fact, communicate in different ways.

2. Whereas strong emotions may be, and often are, blurted out, calmer ones usually require a degree of delicacy for their expression.

3. Men are more literal-minded, for literalness is a mark of logical thinking.

4. Both sexes must be careful not to use their special faculties oppressively. Women must not resort to emotional black-mail. And men must not use logic relentlessly, to force a reluctant agreement.

5. Women are more apt to reject reason altogether, if their feelings don't support a logical trend. Men, on the other hand, are apt to reject feelings altogether *unless* they support such a trend.

6. Communication between the sexes is not only an art to be developed for the sake of harmony in the home. It is also important as a means of rounding out one's own character.

7. Show appreciation, when you feel it. Appreciation is often a more important message than exactness of opinion. No one wants to feel that every day in the home is like sitting for an exam.

8. Don't assume telepathic communication, even when you sometimes have it.

9. Don't assume shared tastes. Rather, pay your spouse the com-pliment of not knowing his or her every wish in advance.

10. Don't assume the other person knows how you feel.

11. Assume *a desire* on your spouse's part for communication and understanding.

12. Listen to the other person at least as often as you want the other to listen to you.

13. In any difference of opinion, don't insist on getting the last word. To give your spouse the last word—lovingly, not sarcastically—is itself a kind of victory.

14. Never play power games. Even if you feel slighted, maintain a noble attitude—not by endeavoring to show your partner how noble *you* are, but by showing complete acceptance and respect.

15. Avoid, if possible, voicing negative emotions.

16. Learn to enjoy silence together. Make your silences communicative, and not mere lapses in the conversation.

17. Pay attention to the tones of your voice. Remember, the way you say something is as important as what you say.

18. Learn to speak more with the eyes. Nobody likes to converse with a talking mask.

19. Hold realistic expectations of one another. Don't expect perfection of your partner. Imperfection is, after all, inherent in the human race.

20. Make courtesy a normal part of your self-expression.

21. Be slow to judge, but ever quick to forgive.

Chapter Ten

Keeping the Wheels
Well Oiled

The machine age has given us many excellent metaphors. Poetic souls may lament the soullessness of it all, but what better metaphor, indeed, for smooth relationships than the well-oiled wheel? And what better, for relationships that grind harshly together, than the wheel direly in need of a lubricant?

Granted, grease lacks a certain poetic beauty when used as a metaphor for wedded bliss. Still, we've all experienced the pleasure of a smooth ride.

It is important in any relationship, and far more so in marriage, to pay careful attention to the daily flow of energy. It is important, for example, to understand the importance of giving outward expression to the love you feel inwardly—even if, in some ways, the expression seems superficial compared to the depth of your feelings.

✺ Mutual Loyalty ✺

The true foundation of every marriage is mutual loyalty. Loyalty can be expressed in many ways. The essential point is that it never be taken for granted.

Don't, for example, try to "score off" your partner by disagreeing with him or her before friends. I have seen couples actually hold each other up to the ridicule of their guests. Genuine humor is of course harmless, but it is not humor when your words conceal a barb. If there is actual disagreement between you, better express it in private.

On the other hand, don't try hypocritically to impress others with a harmony that you make no effort to foster in the privacy of the home.

Loyalty should be a heartfelt commitment; outer demonstrations of your commitment are of secondary importance. Still, to demonstrate it *is* important, for demonstration is the oil which ensures that the wheels of your relationship will keep turning without a squeak.

One demonstration of loyalty is expressed in a vow that I wrote for a marriage ceremony, which I've included at the end of this book. The vow states, "I will never compete with you." It isn't that friendly competition is wrong. In fact, it can be enjoyable, and can even strengthen your relationship, lending it a certain sweetness and humor. Serious competition, however, is another matter. Never let your marriage become a battleground where one partner seeks power advantages over the other.

⚘ Accepting Your Partner ⚘

Another point to remember is this: *Criticism is corrosive.*

I once read in a book words to this effect: "Women marry with the thought, 'He will change.' Men marry with the thought, 'She won't change.' Both are doomed to disappointment." There is much wisdom in those words.

Learn to accept your partner as he or she is. Don't try to *impose* your own notions of what is right or wrong. The best way to change another person is to inspire him to *want* to change. The best way to inspire people to change themselves is to encourage them in their strengths, not to discourage them with constant references to their weaknesses. And the best way to encourage them in their strengths is to be strong in them, yourself.

There is a delightful story about Mahatma Gandhi. A mother, accompanied by her son, once asked Gandhi to tell the little boy not to eat so many sweets. Advice from the great leader of the Indian people would, after all, be taken seriously!

"Ask me again in a week," replied the mahatma.

A week later, the mother, once more accompanied by her son, approached him again. This time, Gandhi turned to the boy and said, "Don't eat so many sweets."

The woman was astonished. Why had it taken him so long to prepare such a simple statement? "Couldn't you have said that to him a week ago?" she asked.

"No," Gandhi replied. "You see, a week ago I was eating sweets, myself."

◈ The Need for Compromise ◈

What if, instead of criticizing, you find yourself being criticized? If you realize that some trait or mannerism of yours is displeasing to your spouse, reflect; see if it isn't something that you'd be willing to change. So long as your principles are not threatened, why not compromise?

The need for compromise is one of the first things to accept in a marriage. Many people consider any compromise a "sell-out"—a surrender of values and principles. This is rarely the case. To refuse to adjust one's personality to the demands or the expectations of another, or to the exigencies of circumstance, is to be pig-headed. Some people even create a sort of mystique around their pig-headedness: They picture themselves, perhaps, as one of those craggy, uncommunicative, and thoroughly unpleasant heroes of an Ayn Rand novel. Even crags, however, become eroded in time. Egotism, as Paramhansa Yogananda stated, is the death of wisdom.

Compromise isn't easy. Still, it is the only way to grow and mature. Compromise is the only way to become well-balanced, kindly, and wise.

When misunderstandings occur, ask yourself, first, "What can I do to change myself?" To help another person in his development is noble and generous. But to feel *responsible* for another person's development is to add an intolerable burden to your own.

❧ Giving Advice? ❧

Whenever you feel inspired to suggest a personal change in your spouse's comportment, concentrate not on *your* need to make the suggestion, but on your spouse's need, *and* readiness, to receive it. Be respectful of your partner's right to grow in his or her own way. For each of us needs the freedom to make his own mistakes. To be overly protective of others is to deprive them of the opportunity to gain experience in life, and therefore to grow in wisdom.

When counseling anyone, you will find it helpful to tell yourself, "No one *owes* it to me to take my advice." Feel gratified, rather, when anything you say is accepted as worthwhile. Give others the freedom, in other words, to grow in their own way and at their own pace. Isn't that what you really want, yourself?

Never be possessive. A marriage certificate is not a deed of ownership. Possessiveness can be like a creeper, squeezing the life out of the tree around which it twines. A plant grows best when it is given free access to air and sunlight. Human beings, similarly, need the "air" of freedom if they are to develop their own insights, and the "sunlight" of inner inspiration if they are to transform intellectually acquired knowledge into mature wisdom. Without the freedom to grow, in yourself, and to live by your own perceptions of reality, you are robbed of your integrity, and your personality is suffocated.

⚘ Remember the Subtle Magnetism ⚘ Between You

When we look at life superficially, from without, we define our relationships in terms of petty details: the daily routine, the respite from duty—meals, television, hyperactive vacations. It is easy, from this perspective, to overlook the unspoken realities: the subtle magnetism you and your spouse share, for example, that drew you together in the first place.

A George Price cartoon in *The New Yorker* said it well. A tenement flat; plaster cracking off the walls; lines strung up in the kitchen, sagging with laundry; two small boys running through the room playing cowboys and Indians; a distraught woman ironing clothes by the sink, with two small children tugging in opposite directions at her dress. By the window the husband sits in his undervest, playing a trombone. The wife pauses a moment to cry, "Can't you play anything except 'Ah, Sweet Mystery of Life'?"

The poet Wordsworth said it more sweetly: "The world is too much with us."

Never let routine chords dull the melody of your romance. Keep ever alive an awareness of the magnetism you share between you. It is a subtle force, all-too-easily forgotten in the busy-ness of daily life.

Pause awhile, now and again, to enjoy the stillnesses, if they pass between you.

❧ Points to Remember ❧

1. Understand the importance of giving outward expression to the love you feel inwardly—even if, in some ways, the expression seems superficial compared to the depth of your feelings.

2. The true foundation of every marriage is mutual loyalty.

3. Always remember, criticism is corrosive.

4. Learn to accept your partner as he or she is. Don't try to *impose* your own notions of what is right or wrong.

5. The best way to change others is to inspire them to *want* to change themselves.

6. The best way to inspire people to change themselves is to encourage them in their strengths, not to discourage them by constant references to their weaknesses.

7. The best way to encourage others in their strengths is to be strong in them, yourself.

8. The need for compromise is one of the first things to accept in a marriage. To refuse to adjust one's personality to the demands or the expectations of another, or to the exigencies of circumstance, is to be pig-headed.

9. When misunderstandings occur, ask yourself, first, "What can I do to change myself?"

10. Whenever you feel inspired to make a suggestion for your spouse's improvement, concentrate not on your own need to make it, but on his or her need, *and readiness*, to receive it.

11. When counseling anyone, you will find it helpful to tell yourself, "No one *owes* it to me to take my advice." Feel gratified, rather, when anything you say is accepted as worthwhile.

12. Give others the freedom to grow in their own way, and at their own pace. Isn't that what you really want, yourself?

13. Never be possessive. A marriage certificate is not a deed of ownership.

14. Pause awhile, now and then, to enjoy the stillnesses, if they pass between you.

Chapter  Eleven

Expansive Child Raising

The basic principles mentioned so far apply also to the question of raising children. Children, perhaps even more than one's spouse, are incentives that force one to learn to relate *responsibly* to others—to relate, that is, in a giving way, eschewing the thought (so instinctive to the ego), "What's in it for me?"

The marital relationship, too, forces one to relate responsibly. For whatever you say or do has repercussions that it wouldn't have if you were, say, a hermit. Thus in marriage you are disciplined in ways that you might never have been otherwise—in ways that you never are when relating casually to strangers.

For one thing, you are obliged in marriage to relate to another person's ups and downs, and to do so meaningfully and sincerely. Thus, marriage might be compared to two pebbles rolling together down a riverbed, each gradually wearing away rough edges in the other.

But if this is true of marriage, how much more true is it of your relationship with your children. After all, you can make demands of your spouse, up to a point. But how many can you make of your children? In times of tragedy, you and your spouse may offer comfort to one another; rarely, however, will your children be aware enough, and strong enough, to give *you* comfort. When facing major trials or challenges, husband and wife can stand together. But how much help are children under such circumstances? More often, they are a liability.

❧ Give, Give, and Give ❧

Children *are* a comfort, in other ways. They are also a joy, a hope for the future—many things: but a bulwark of strength?—almost never. And so it is that parents raising their children must learn to give—and give, and give! It is a wonderful opportunity, like the challenge of marriage itself, but one—again, like marriage—that must be approached selflessly, and with wisdom.

In the divine scheme where marriage is concerned, matrimony itself helps us, or at least challenges us, to expand our sympathies. It does so, in the first place, by appealing to our natural desire for personal fulfillment, and, in the second, by expanding that desire to include the welfare of one other human being: our wife or husband.

Offspring, when they come, expand our sympathies further by adding to the family circle, and by giving us even less opportunity for focusing on *personal* fulfillment.

As our children grow toward maturity, and gradually wean themselves from the family nest, our sympathies continue to expand through *their* expanding interests. Even thereafter, we can continue to demolish mental barriers by expanding our sympathies at last to include all humanity.

The struggle for self-expansion is not equally difficult at every stage: from self to spouse, from spouse to children, from children to neighbors, from neighbors to countrymen, from countrymen to humanity everywhere, and even beyond humanity—outward to the universe. Once the barrier of personal attachment has been broken—once, in other words, we learn to expand our love beyond the petty enclosure of "I and mine," it becomes relatively easy to expand it ever further, until it embraces all.

Wisest, finally, is that person who doesn't wait for the natural order to *push* him forward on the pathway to enlightenment. Knowing that the right direction is toward self-expansion, he doesn't wait passively for the process to happen automatically. Why, indeed, wait years to live *through* others, when life at every moment calls us to expand our own self-identity?

❧ God in Disguise ❧

The wisest approach to child raising is to recognize in every child from the beginning, not a creation of our own, but a newcomer to the home: God, come to remind us of Himself, and of *His* love for us. In this way it becomes easier to break the powerful hypnosis of delusion (again, that old "I and mine"), and to bring to our family life most perfectly the realization that *all* belongs to Him.

Without the respect that allows others complete freedom to develop, each at his own rate and in his own way, it is all but impossible for people truly to expand their relationships. Always there will arise the temptation to make selfish demands of one another.

In the raising of children, especially, it is important to remember that they are already-developed souls, come into your family as guests. You have a responsibility to share with them your greater experience of life, perhaps your wisdom, certainly your love and protection. But you have *no* right to expect them to grow up as *reflections* of your personality and your ambitions.

Most of us behold only the child. Observing his innocence, we imagine that he has everything to learn from us. Yet who knows with what wisdom he has come, "trailing clouds of glory," as Wordsworth wrote in "Intimations of Immortality." Perhaps even, as some believe, the child has lived on earth before. Should this be true, the child may be as experienced in the ways of this world as we are—even if his experience is, for the present, a little rusty.

Education, in the original Latin, means, "a drawing out." Truly to educate a child, it is necessary to inspire him to respond *from within*. Well has it been said that truths are not so much learned as *recognized*. And while the child seems helpless now, during its efforts to cope with its unaccustomed tools, yet even during these formative years it deserves the respect and consideration due to a soul that is struggling, even as we are, to attain its highest potential.

Indeed, just as it is important to respect your spouse as a manifestation of God, so is it equally important to give that respect to your children.

You'll have to treat them as children too, of course. For a while they are playing the role—more deliberately, perhaps, than you know!—of being helpless and irresponsible. A mother I know, in endeavoring to toilet train her three-year-old, tried to shame him with that old ploy, "Come on, be a *big* boy!"

"I don't want to be a big boy," he replied. "I *like* being a baby!"

It's a game they play for a time, you see. And they'll force you to play it with them.

But just see how responsibly even a six-year-old can behave if his parents die, leaving him to take care of his three-year-old sister. In many ways—and how astonishingly!—he will seem to grow up overnight.

Children know more than they let on. And sometimes, in fact, they do let on.

My mother tells of how one day she was sitting at her dressing table, putting on make-up. I watched for a while, then said to her in all seriousness, "Mother, don't be always thinking of your beauty, like Mrs. M———"; here I named someone who was, in fact, inordinately vain. It was an observation my mother hadn't expected to hear from a little child.

Children do understand. But they may prefer not to call upon that more mature knowledge, perhaps because they find it more fun, for a while, not to have to face the burdens that come with adulthood. (Hence the perennial appeal of Peter Pan, the legendary boy who never grew up.)

So, respect your children—as developed souls in undeveloped bodies and minds, and also as possessing the full right, as children, to be childish—even foolish sometimes, perhaps even completely out of control. Every age is burdened with its attendant follies. Recognize your own in that parade of weaknesses, and give others the freedom to wean themselves from their own, as and when they elect to do so.

If you respect your children's freedom to play their chosen roles, they will respond to you in kind, giving *you* respect. Parents who talk down to their children find the resultant frustration of their offspring emerging, eventually, in the form of rebellion.

A United Front

The principle of loyalty to one's own first, then expanding that loyalty to include others as one's own, should be expressed in the family by showing loyalty to your spouse first, and only within that framework of loyalty, to your children.

A father I know had just told his daughter that she could not have more cookies from a tray. Just then the mother came onto the scene.

"Mommy," cried the little girl, through wheedling tears, "Daddy won't let me have any more cookies!"

"Well," said the mother conciliatingly, "you may have just one more."

One more! She might as well have given her the whole trayful. Already the message had been conveyed: "Don't listen to Daddy. Listen to me."

Parents must support each other in disciplining their children. Even if you think your spouse is mistaken, you cannot afford to present a divided front to your children.

Of course, I am referring here to situations where discipline is involved. If, instead, the husband says that Venus is in the evening sky, and the wife happens to know that it is Mercury, what is the harm of pointing out his error? By a parental example of harmonious disagreement the children may even receive a valuable lesson in how to handle similar situations in their own lives.

But when it comes to disciplining them, remember that, however ignorant they may be in other departments, when it comes to politics they are masters! Somehow they understand the art from the very cradle. They know perfectly how to divide and conquer. And even before they have learned to speak, they know how to play upon your emotions in order to get what they want. So, if feasible, and without suppressing their actual needs, keep a united front! Be loyal first of all to each other.

❧ Act in Fairness, Not in Anger ❧

Another very important point with children is to be absolutely fair with them. Never address them in anger. That isn't always easy! I remember an occasion when I was a child. My family was visiting relatives. Dad was dressed in his Sunday best, eating breakfast prior to going to church. Little Eddie, my smart-aleck cousin, was sitting next to him. Suddenly Eddie's voice piped up, "Uncle Ray, I'm putting oatmeal on your coat." And he was, too, in thick layers. Dad's anger was, I think, understandable. And anger was probably the only reaction Eddie would have understood.

Let's face it, children can sometimes drive you nuts! Sometimes, in fact, that is their entire intention. But remember, if you respond to them too often in kind, you'll lose your hold on them. They'll test you, to see if they can drag you down to their level of immaturity, but if ever they succeed, they will never again give you the respect that is an adult's due.

Always, then, speak to them with justice. Be fair. Be impartial. In this way you may scold them, severely even—and sometimes you may need to; you can't always be shining through with sweetness and light—and still you'll have their respect.

Furthermore, even if you speak scoldingly, if you do so with love in your heart, you'll still have their love.

I have mentioned that I lived for several years with the great teacher, Paramhansa Yogananda. Sometimes it happened that he had to scold us, his adult children, in order to get a message to sink through our thick skulls. Whenever he did so, I always saw love in his eyes.

A little boy runs out into a street crowded with traffic. How will you handle the situation? Will you call out to him sweetly, "Come back, Johnny. You might get run over"? Certainly not! You'll grab him by the scruff of the neck, perhaps give him a good wallop to make sure you impress it on him never to do such a thing again, and make very sure in any way you can that he gets the message once and forever.

Adults aren't used to being spoken to in this way. Once one realizes, however, that full maturity isn't something one attains at eighteen or twenty-one—that it means wisdom and the perfection of true soul-qualities, and that an arduous and long apprenticeship is necessary if one is to attain true understanding—one gladly embraces any discipline life throws at him, for it helps him to grow spiritually.

Life itself contrives to teach us many lessons the hard way. Scolding from a wise teacher may impress on a disciple the need for changing a course of behavior that might otherwise bring him great suffering. Considered as an alternative to that suffering, the scolding—like that of the parent whose child has run out into traffic—is a demonstration of pure love. And that, as I said, is what I saw in Yogananda's eyes on the few occasions when he scolded me. I saw regret, deep concern for my welfare, and unconditional love.

Sometimes, then, to make a point, you may have to resort to strong discipline. But whenever you do so, never, ever convey the message that you are speaking or acting out of personal rancor. If you do, your child will feel your emotion, and remember it long afterwards as that time when you allowed a fleeting situation to take precedence over your love for him. Such memories can be traumatic in the development of a child, even as they sometimes are in the life of an adult.

A related point to the above is this one: Never, in any loving relationship, allow the people involved to assume secondary importance, in your eyes, to the outward circumstances of your relationship. *People are more important than things.*

To Spank or Not to Spank

Should you ever spank your child? Many parents are so opposed to this practice that they wax angry if the question is merely raised. But I think we have to take into account the personalities of individual children.

Some children are more identified with their bodies than others. They may sometimes, then, need to have their lessons administered in a physical manner; otherwise, they may not heed them at all. Other children are more mental in their outlook on life. To such children, a lesson administered physically may be considered a great indignity.

In my own family, I was the thinker; my brother Bob was the doer. If ever Bob got spanked, he forgot about it immediately; no trauma was involved. Sometimes, indeed, it was the best way of getting through to him, though spankings in any case were rare in our family. For myself, the only time I remember being spanked *was* traumatic. Weeks later, I looked at my father and demanded of him, "Why did you spank me?" Fortunately, he realized immediately that it hadn't been the right way to get through to me, and never spanked me again.

In fairness to my father, I should add that he was always scrupulously fair. It was above all his sense of justice that impressed his lessons on our minds. These qualities are, I believe, what all children respect most. Parents who "fly off the handle" simply to release their own emotions end up not being listened to at all.

"Oh, there's old Dad, blowing off again!" You will win your children's respect only if you make justice the basis of any discipline you administer—particularly if the justice is directed toward what is right and best for them.

They will respect and love you if, above all, you temper justice with kindness. They'll respond more to love even than to justice. We all need mercy occasionally. Let them know that you are on their side—that you are their friend.

⚜ Limits and Broad Horizons ⚜

It is important also, of course, to let them know that you won't stand for any nonsense. You must be firm. Children, you see, are always trying to test their outer limits. And if you keep backing off out of blind love for them, they'll end up becoming spoiled.

What does it mean to be spoiled? It means to grow up with the thought that, somehow—if necessary by throwing tantrums—one can always get one's own way in life. It means to become divorced from objective reality by always living a dream. It means being unable to relate to any point of view but one's own. What a constricted world to live in, indeed!

Such an attitude is the very opposite of self-expansion. It is the very surest road to later unhappiness, as an adult.

Children need the sense of security that comes from knowing what their limits are. They need to feel that, within any given mental enclosure, the territory is unassailably theirs. But from that secure base they also need to be allowed—indeed, encouraged—gradually to expand their horizons.

The trick is not to impose that expansion on them, but to invite them to seek it for themselves.

The trick also is not to impose your own limitations on them (like parents, for instance, who don't want their musically gifted child to practice the piano because the sound bothers them). If you restrain them unnaturally, you will stifle their development.

It is important, then, to develop a feeling for the potentials of each child; then, within the limits of those potentials, to try sensitively to get him to accept ever-broader horizons.

If you are, truly, a loving parent, this will mean also weaning your child gradually from dependence on home and family. Sooner or later he will have to go out anyway, to face the world on his own. Why not prepare him for that independence?

⚘ Developing Independence ⚘ in Your Child

Children need security. But if you give them too much of it, you won't help them. If you give them too much money, for example, you may spoil them. If you make life too easy for them, they won't understand that life itself is filled with challenges. In these ways you can spoil them even after they grow up.

Yogananda said that wealthy people who leave too much money to their children make a great mistake—at least until such a time as those "children" become *mature* adults, successful in their own right.

Parents who can afford to might give their offspring enough money to get started in life and to stand on their own feet, but not enough to encourage dependence. Your children may not thank you, in the beginning, for teaching them the benefits of austerity, but they'll certainly be grateful later on.

Try also to put your children on their own feet emotionally as soon as possible. How soon? A friend of mine, returning from India recently, had made an interesting observation there. She'd been astonished never to see a child crying. That is to say, as soon as a child under the age of about two began to cry, its mother would lift it onto her lap and cuddle it. The sense of security this attention induced in the child kept it serene. Here in America it may be that we try to wean them from that security too early.

So when I speak of weaning them emotionally, I mean to wean them at their own natural pace, with sensitivity to *their* rhythms. Some children actually want to be weaned sooner. Others are more psychologically dependent, and may need a slower approach. Always, take into account the child's individuality.

As a general rule—I have explained this point more carefully in my book, *Education for Life*—the first six years are a period of utter dependence; the next six, of only slowly diminishing dependence. By the time a child reaches his teens, it is normally time to encourage him to discipline himself and to stand on his own feet.

Try always, above all, to direct the development of your children toward an expanding view of the true meaning of family—not the "us four and no more" consciousness, but the acceptance of all beings as their broader family.

❧ Points to Remember ❧

1. The wisest approach to child raising is to recognize in every child from the beginning, not a creation of our own, but a newcomer to the home: God, come to remind us of Himself and of *His* love for us.

2. Education, in the original Latin, means "a drawing out." Truly to educate a child, it is necessary to inspire him to respond from *within*.

3. Children understand, but they may prefer not to call upon that more mature knowledge, perhaps because they find it more fun for a while not to have to face the burdens that come with adulthood.

4. If you respect your children's freedom to play the role they choose to play, they will respond to you in kind, giving *you* respect.

5. Be absolutely fair with your children. Never address them in anger.

6. Children test you, to see if they can drag you down to their level of immaturity. But if ever they succeed, they will never again give you the respect that is an adult's due.

7. Children will respect and love you if, above all, you temper justice with kindness. Let them know you are on their side—that you are their friend.

8. Children are always trying to test their outer limits. If you keep backing off out of blind love for them, they'll end up spoiled. They need the sense of security that comes from knowing what their limits are. They need to feel that, within any given mental enclosure, the territory is unassailably theirs.

9. The trick is not to impose expansion on them, but to invite them to seek it for themselves.

10. It is important to develop a feeling for the potentials of each child, and then, within the limits of those potentials, to try sensitively to wean him to an acceptance of ever-broader horizons. If you are, truly, a loving parent, this will mean also weaning your child from dependence on its home and family.

11. Children need security. If you give it to them in suffocating measures, however, you will only stifle their development.

12. Parents who can afford to might give their offspring enough money to help them get started in life, and to stand on their own feet, but not enough to encourage dependence.

13. Try always, above all, to direct the development of your children toward an acceptance of all beings as their broader family.

Chapter Twelve

Expansive Marriage

One of the false expectations with which many couples approach marriage is that they will be, forever, all in all to each other. I can't visualize *any* two people remaining satisfied for long with this thought, unless they are exceptionally dull. No one person is ever going to help you learn all your lessons in life. No one person is going to fulfill your every need: no one, that is, but yourself.

For all the fulfillment you have ever sought awaits you within. But that kind of fulfillment is never personal, for it transcends the ego.

One purpose of marriage is, as I've said earlier, to give people an incentive to expand their self-identity. By loving one other person we learn to break, to some extent at least, our ego-bondage. Once we've established self-expansion as our direction of development, it is easier to continue the process, broadening our affections to include other people, other races, other nations—the world.

To fix this expansive image more clearly in your mind, imagine a particular wave on the ocean as being endowed with a personality. This wave, concentrating on its own special reality, decides that only that which happens to it, out of all the waves on the ocean, has meaning for it.

Think of this wave, then, as pushing itself up ever higher in its self-importance, until it imagines it can dominate all the surrounding waves. It takes a strong wind, however, for a wave to rise high. Where one wave rises up, others will rise also. Thus, the wave finds itself increasingly threatened by other waves, each with a personality of its own, and each inflated, similarly, with a sense of its own importance. As the first wave tries to dominate all the waves around it, so they, too, strive for dominion. Thus, conflict develops among these self-seeking waves. Clashing together in arrogance and ambition, they experience fear, pain, and suffering.

People are like those waves. The more a person affirms his own self-importance, the greater is his desire to promote and protect his ego, and the greater the pain he experiences—and the more fleeting his pleasures.

There is no escape from suffering, so long as people seek their escape *through* the ego. The way to liberation lies in withdrawing the ego-wave back into the infinite ocean. It lies in realizing that its own greater reality is the reality of the ocean. To expand one's awareness beyond the ego is no loss, though the ego perceives it as such and fights against it with all the skill at its command.

Marriage is one step toward breaking our attachment to the pettiness of ego-dominion. It is a step, but for many a vital one, toward soul-expansion. For anything that helps a person to break out of the confines of selfishness and self-seeking is good. Anything that further enmeshes a person in ego-consciousness is bad, imprisoning him in pain and limitation. It is bad, in short, because it is bad *for him*.

Since marriage is one means whereby people gain an incentive to learn self-expansion, marriage is a holy institution. It has a much higher purpose than mere selfish fulfillment.

If marriage is not viewed in this light, it can become a barrier to true fulfillment. Couples who marry only for self-gratification reinforce their contractive tendency, and strengthen their egos. Couples, again, who give lovingly to each other, but enclose themselves against further expansion, build walls around their little, shared reality that, by shutting out others, have a contractive effect on their own consciousness.

For life cannot exist without movement. Movement that is not expansive will be contractive. Life cannot hold a static pose for long. Even in the stillness of stagnation there is evaporation, and the proliferation of noxious insects.

❧ The Adventure of Self-Awakening ❧

Life is an adventure in self-awakening. Anything that stands in the way of this process is, in the end, damaging, because stultifying. To those who seek true fulfillment in their lives, marriage should be seen not as a cozy nook, but as a window opening onto ever-expanding realities.

For many people, marriage represents a reinforcement of their natural egoic tendencies. It represents an attempt to buttress their fragile sense of security and self-worth. But for those who approach life in an adventurous spirit—for those who seek constant self-expansion—marriage represents a glorious opportunity for self-development.

Selfish people marry for what they can get from one another. Generous people marry for what they can *share* with one another. Consciously or unconsciously, generous people realize that their greatest gain lies in expanding their sympathies, not in limiting them.

Selfish people think, "What can I get out of this relationship?" Generous people think, "What can I *give* to this relationship?"

Needless to say, the world is not divided simplistically into two distinct camps. People grow, moreover, beyond their first understanding. What we must emphasize in our lives is not the stage to which we have arrived so far, but the direction our journey must take us in future.

To refer to people too glibly, then, as "selfish" or "generous" would be a mistake. People are complex. People change. The important thing is to be aware of specific *directions* of growth.

The more a person's sympathies expand outward, the greater his or her fulfillment. And the more those sympathies shrink inward upon the ego—or, what is almost the same thing, upon their own family with the thought of "I and mine"—the more deeply that person experiences insecurity and a gnawing sense of unfulfillment.

An emphasis on universality is not for those people who haven't learned first the importance of loyalty to one's own. The husband who thinks, "I love all—so why be faithful to my wife?" has yet to develop the refinement needed for understanding the kind of expansion I am describing. True self-expansion means escaping bondage to the ego. What the libertine accomplishes, on the contrary, is the strengthening of his ego-bonds.

It isn't only charity, then, that begins at home: Loyalty begins there, too. Only through the windows of loyalty can one reach out and touch others—as, on deep levels of our consciousness, all of us really want to do.

Here, then, is a way to make your marriage expansive in the best sense. The method requires meditation and introspection—or, to put it differently, it requires really getting to know yourself, on ever deeper levels.

Learn to love yourself in the soul way, by perceiving in meditation the hidden joy of your own being. Then, with a love decreasingly selfish, reach out to touch your spouse, your children. Refine your love so that it becomes ever more pure, containing less and less of the consciousness of "I and mine." Love your family as you ought to love yourself: for their souls, not only for their bodies and personalities.

Then expand that love outward to include your neighbors, your countrymen, all mankind, and all sentient beings—everywhere. In this way your love will expand to become the love of God.

An outward expansion of love is what Yogananda called the social way of attaining cosmic consciousness. And a very important balance it is to the inner path of seeking union with God in meditation.

Marriage can be a doorway, in both an outer and an inner sense, to infinite awareness. But it will only become that if you work hard at making it so. The obstacles to success are many. While facing those obstacles as you struggle toward perfection, remember further these words: "There are no such things as obstacles: There are only opportunities!"

In describing spiritual marriage, I want to emphasize this final point: that marriage, as such, is in no way a panacea; it is what you *do* with marriage that determines whether you will progress toward greater freedom, or regress toward an increase of those delusions which, all your life, have brought you pain. The greater your inner freedom, the greater will be your happiness, and the deeper and more fulfilling your love.

≫ Points to Remember ≪

1. There is no escape from suffering, so long as people seek their escape through the ego.

2. Anything that further enmeshes a person in ego-consciousness is bad, for it imprisons him in pain and limitation. It is bad, in short, because it is bad *for him*.

3. Since marriage is one means whereby people are given an incentive to learn self-expansion, marriage is a holy institution.

4. Life cannot exist without movement. Movement that is not expansive will be contractive.

5. Life is an adventure in self-awakening. Anything that stands in the way of this process is, in the end, damaging, because stultifying.

6. An emphasis on universality is not for those people who haven't learned first the importance of loyalty to one's own.

7. The way to make your marriage expansive in the best sense is through meditation and introspection.

8. When you face obstacles in your struggle toward perfection, remember these words: "There are no such things as obstacles: There are only opportunities."

9. Marriage, as such, is in no way a panacea; it is what you *do* with marriage that determines what you will get out of it.

10. The greater your inner freedom, the greater will be your happiness, and the deeper and more fulfilling, your love.

Chapter Thirteen

For Those Who Are
Seeking God

I conclude with a few thoughts on marriage for those who are consciously on the spiritual path. I say *consciously* because everyone in the world, whether aware of the fact or not, is on the spiritual path. And I say *the*, rather than *a*, path to emphasize the truth that life itself constitutes a process of spiritual evolution from inchoate to ever higher awareness. Since everyone is, in this sense, on the spiritual path, this chapter ought theoretically to be for everybody. But in fact it asks more of most people than they would be ready to give. *Caveat emptor!* Take what I've written here only if it appeals to you.

For those who are consciously seeking self-realization, the rules change. The sincere devotee no longer needs reasons for spiritualizing his awareness. He knows already that a better way exists than the usual battle for worldly gain and recognition. Like an athlete, rather, in training for the Big Event, the heart of the devotee is bent on spiritual victory. He or she, if married, accepts as the fundamental guideline in that marriage the need to attune every act to the Divine Will. Because renunciation of egoic desires forms the basis of the spiritual life, regardless of a person's outer calling, I shall compare frequently, in this chapter, the path of the spiritually seeking householder to that of the outwardly declared renunciate, which tradition defines as the spiritual life.

In the early editions of *Autobiography of a Yogi* (Chapter 24), Paramhansa Yogananda drew a comparison between the householder path and that of monastic renunciation. "To fulfill one's earthly responsibilities," he wrote, "is indeed the higher path, provided the yogi, maintaining a mental uninvolvement with egotistical desires, plays his part as a willing instrument of God." He did not mean, of course, that marriage is *in itself* "the higher path." The sincere seeker, if contemplating marriage as a path to God, must be prepared resolutely to leave the beaten track of ego-gratification.

St. Paul tells us in I Corinthians: "He that is unmarried careth for the things that belong to the Lord, how he may please the Lord: but he that is married careth for the things of the world, how he may please his wife." Paramhansa Yogananda, quoting this passage also, went on to say, "I had analyzed the lives of many of my friends who, after undergoing certain spiritual discipline, had then married. Launched on the sea of worldly responsibilities, they had forgotten their resolutions to meditate deeply. To allot God a secondary place in life was, to me, inconceivable."

✺ God First ✺

The important thing, in a marriage committed to spiritual development, is to allot God the *primary* place in life. It is to seek diminishing involvement with the "things of the world." It is to seek to please God first, and one's wife or husband secondarily. The spiritual seeker who is married must, like the renunciate, do his best "to maintain a mental uninvolvement with egotistical desires." He must play his part "as a willing instrument of God."

The transformation from "sinner" to saint is never accomplished easily, under any circumstances. Monks and nuns as well as householders are easily inclined to try to please others first, and indeed have more people around them to please. They, too, must struggle valiantly "to maintain a mental un-involvement with egotistical desires." Nor is it easy for any-one, whatever his role in life, to "play his part as a willing instrument of God."

The difficulty in marriage, specifically, is the need to ac-cept that one's partner may have desires that need honor-ing even while one strives, personally, to develop non-at-tachment. On the other hand, to try to please others while offering one's personal desires to God can be an excellent ex-ercise in discrimination, as well as in self-abnegation.

The more difficult a task, the greater, often, the rewards. The challenge for renunciates and householders is essentially the same: to develop an inner sanctuary in the mind. People confuse outwardly religious deeds with spirituality. Brother Lawrence, however, in his famous book, *The Practice of the Presence of God*, stated that he had reached a point in his spir-itual life where he felt as much devotion when picking up a straw as while at worship in the chapel. What was so par-ticularly meaningful to him about picking up straws? Noth-ing, obviously. It was his *attitude of devotion* that gave the act meaning. When a person's mind is internalized, he perceives God's presence everywhere, and in everything.

Monks and nuns are, in the popular imagination, im-mersed constantly in divine inspiration, whereas household-ers are considered, almost by definition, to be immersed in the pursuit of personal desires and of ego-fulfillment. The truth of the matter in both cases may be very different.

Some years ago I visited the Greek island of Patmos, where St. John wrote the Book of Revelation. At the time of my de-parture, as I and others were awaiting the ship, a French lady in the line ahead of me exclaimed, "I had the blessing of talking with some of the nuns in the monastery here. Ah, what peace they emanated!"

"Really?" I remarked. "I met a few of the monks, but I must say I didn't find them all that peaceful."

"Well,"—the lady paused reflectively and laughed—"now that you mention it, the nuns didn't seem all that peaceful, either!"

She had allowed her expectations, no doubt formed in a convent school, to color her perceptions.

Social conditioning stands in the way also of spiritualizing people's understanding of marriage. Married couples are *expected* to be motivated by self-interest. Everyone, including many monks and nuns, supports this expectation, causing couples to feel that it must be somehow morally wrong for them to live for higher principles.

❧ A Householder Devotee ❧

Social norms often are based, not on truth, but on accumulations of fantasy. In answer to this particular fantasy, let me offer a recollection of my own mother. Gertrude Walters was in many ways a very normal housewife. Yet she loved God, and did her best to live a life pleasing to Him. Though not, perhaps, "heroic" in her dedication, she was steadfast in it. Her life was, I imagine, typical of many householders who quietly and unostentatiously offer their lives to God—as Mother did my life also, during what was her first pregnancy. In Mother's case, many people were amazed to observe that, the older she grew, the more beautiful she became.

During her lifetime I never heard anyone speak of her in any terms other than the highest praise. There was something about her that no one really understood, but that charmed all whom she met. The wife of Georges Enesco, the Romanian composer, called her "*un être esquis*"—an exquisite being.

Yet there was nothing wraithlike or unreal about my mother. She was incapable of striking a pose—unless, indeed, occasionally, in humorous imitation of some attitude that she deplored. For, yes, she *was* capable of deploring, though she almost always did so humorously. She could be wryly critical of anyone who pretended to be "other-worldly," for example. For she was also a woman of firm common sense. Her devotion was a thing she kept very private. Outwardly a supportive and loving wife, a good mother, a charming hostess, and a conscientious homemaker who could fret that she had "absolutely ruined tonight's dinner!" (when to the rest of us it always tasted delicious), she set time apart secretly every day to pray and meditate.

I don't suppose it was anything she did, outwardly, that made her so special. Rather, it was what she *was*. She had a virtue comparable to "picking up straws" with devotion.

Was she a saint? Few, I imagine, would even think to ask the question. Yet I remember an occasion years after her death. It was the anniversary of her birthday, and I had been planning to say a special prayer for her. Unfortunately, on that day I was afflicted with such a rapid heartbeat that I found it difficult to think of anything beyond my physical discomfort. Late that night, to my own surprise, I found myself praying *to* her, rather than *for* her. An instant later I was healed.

⚡ New Definitions Are Needed ⚡

For many householders, the greatest obstacle to living more spiritually lies in the simple thought, "But what can I *do* that is all that spiritual?" The difficulty lies in the thought that spirituality demands *doing* things that are commonly labeled "spiritual." And it lies in the definitions people accept of the householder state. The need of the age is for new definitions, leading to new expectations.

And the time is ripe for them. For a new consciousness has begun to enter the human race, demanding a widespread transformation of outlook. That traditional concepts of marriage no longer work, even for those who believe in "the old ways," is evident in the high prevalence of divorce.

Transformation is needed in every walk of life. The high attrition in monasteries, too, gives evidence of this need. Old concepts of renunciation fail, as old concepts of marriage fail, to embrace the expansive awareness of this age of energy-consciousness into which we have emerged after centuries of matter- and form-consciousness. In monasteries, the joy of living for God must replace the traditional emphasis on suffering. Love and gratitude must be emphasized over self-reproach and self-punishment. The present volume is not the place, obviously, to discuss the present-day needs of monasteries. My point here is that the entire spiritual path needs to be understood in new ways, in order to match the present-day needs of those who, regardless of their outward life-styles, want to live a life centered in God. Marriage and home life, too, offer a vast and untapped potential for people who feel drawn to seek God in a more normal setting than that of the monastery.

Householders can indeed be God-seeking devotees, once they understand that to worship God truly is, simply and basically, to *love* Him, and not necessarily to participate in specific outward forms of service to Him. Everything a person does can become, in that sense, a divine work. For every human life is part of a sweeping divine drama. It is merely easier to see one's work as spiritual when it is given the outward clothing of some spiritual cause.

The essential difference between the life of a householder devotee and that of formal renunciation lies in the fact that householders are obliged to accept the differences between the sexes, and to build on those differences, as opposed to denying their self-identity as men or women. Because the ultimate goal of spiritual striving is to rise above egoic involvement in the realization of union with God, the goal of the householder devotee cannot be radically different in any respect from that of the monk or nun. Marriage, for the devotee, cannot be taken as a license for sexual over-indulgence. I shall refrain from restating in this chapter the merits of sexual self-control. I hope the point was made adequately earlier. As far as sex is concerned, for the householder devotee the maxim holds true, "Less is more."

Why marry at all, then? Because such is the way of nature. Because, for most people, sexual desire can be more easily transcended by gradual degrees than all at once. Because there are gains to be achieved in uniting opposite but complementary natures, gains that might be sacrificed by rejecting this outward inducement to inner balance.

Just as householders are in danger, in working to create a home together, of forgetting their spiritual goals, so monks and nuns are in danger of losing their spiritual balance by avoidance of marriage: the danger of suppressing, rather than transcending, their human natures, and of becoming emotionally cold and unsympathetic—or, conversely, subject to unreasonable outbursts of emotion. They may risk becoming dependent on dry reason for their understanding, rather than on the smooth flow of intuition.

Which path is better: that of the householder or the renunciate? The choice must be left to the individual. Human nature is too varied to admit of absolute rules. For householder devotees, however, it is obvious that monastic attitudes toward sex cannot apply. I am referring not to the sex act itself, but to the simple attraction between two persons of opposite sexes. I have seen too many couples, in their attempt to create a spiritual marriage, try to model their relationship on attitudes that, while right and proper in the monastic life, are abnormal in marriage. Torn between attraction on the one hand, and guilt-ridden rejection on the other, they succeed only in developing complexes both in themselves and in their relationship together.

৯\ Perfecting Our Human Natures /৵

There is a natural balance that ensues from a healthy relationship between husband and wife: the harmonizing of reason and feeling. The renunciate, foregoing this opportunity, must work to achieve it in himself, or else to rise above human nature altogether. Ideally, his consciousness should be centered not in his personality, but in the superconscious flow of intuition in the spine. The perfect renunciate lives not in the realm of likes and dislikes, but as an egoless channel for the divine.

For householders to attempt to deny human nature would be both unrealistic and counterproductive. There is, indeed, already too much of an attempt in modern society to explain away the differences between men and women, as though these differences didn't exist. The result of this unisex attitude has not been clarity, but confusion: women trying to be like men; men behaving either in an aggressively masculine manner or, conversely, striving to suppress their masculinity; widespread homosexuality (often the result of the debasement of sexual attraction to a purely biological function); and a state of constant war between the sexes.

Husbands in relation to their wives need to strive to perfect the divine aspect of their own masculinity. And wives in relation to their husbands need, similarly, to strive to perfect in themselves the divine aspects of femininity.

People need role models. Lacking worthwhile ones, they are misled by countless false examples. The tough, taciturn, or aggressive male; the emotionally explosive, seductively passionate, or timidly clinging female: these are but a few of the heroes and heroines that are offered to the movie-going or book-reading public as ideals. Other examples abound, but few or none today are helpful, spiritually. Where can couples turn to learn how to behave? In marriage, as in most fields of modern life, new models are needed.

❧ The Ideal Husband and Wife ❧

The ideal couple for all time was depicted in the *Ramayana*, a great Indian epic written thousands of years ago. Rama epitomized the ideal husband; Sita, the ideal wife. Their examples are still valid today.

Rama displayed the masculine nature developed to perfection. He was high-minded, magnanimous, unhesitatingly truthful, strong in himself, committed at all times to what was right and true, ever ready to protect and defend the weak, forgiving of weakness in others, generous in victory, firmly committed to virtue, demanding of no one, fair-minded, reasonable, and wise.

Sita was divine perfection manifested as femininity: loving, compassionate, utterly loyal, supportive, motherly, self-sacrificing; the counterpart of Rama in every virtue, but with softness and all-inclusive understanding rather than with outward strength.

Each saw in the other, not the human personality merely, but a manifestation of the Divine. Each delighted in that manifestation in the other, rather than observing the other for deficiencies in himself.

In a dance, a couple twirling together in a circle gain momentum by leaning backward, away from each other. In the relationship between the sexes, similarly, part of its beauty derives from each leaning back, so to speak, into the natural differences that exist between himself, or herself, and his counterpart. Even granting that most of these differences are superficial (we are, after all, the same species); and granting that many of the perceived differences are a sort of myth agreed upon: yet it cannot be denied that our bodies, whether male or female, affect us differently. Husbands and wives, instead of denying those differences, if they aspire to scale the heights of spirituality, would do well to carry those differences to a divine level.

One facet of the relationship between Rama and Sita will, on the face of it, hold little appeal for modern men and women. Sita served her husband, and was obedient to him. Rama, for his part, accepted her service as ennobling both to himself and to her. For him, her obedience was a reminder to himself to live always in the truth. For it was to his expression of the truth that she gave her obedience, not to his human personality. (Indeed, when Rama told her to remain in the palace, instead of following him in his exile in the forest, Sita reminded him lovingly but firmly that her place was by his side. Rama had no choice but to acquiesce.)

❧ Service and Obedience ❧

Service to others has come to be viewed as demeaning. Yet that which diminishes the ego cannot but exalt the soul. Service is a recognized and honored path to God. Monks and nuns serve God through the poor, through the children they teach, or through their monastic superiors. Sita's service to Rama was, as I said, *self*-ennobling. Nor was it that Rama did not serve her. It was only that his service to her was more outward, for her defense and protection.

On the question of obedience, there are wives nowadays who have found it a tool much more effective than nagging for keeping their husbands "on their mettle." The important thing, as Sita understood, is to offer obedience *impersonally*—to truth, rather than to the person.

When feeling submits itself to the judgments of reason, it becomes intuition. When reason understands that feeling wants to be helpful, not to compete, reason listens, and tempers its understanding with intuitive wisdom. The man who is approached with an attitude, "Do you really feel this is right and true?" rather than attacked with such veiled accusations as, "Why do you *always* make this mistake?" is a hundred times more likely to relinquish an unreasonable stand for one that is best for everyone.

The offering up of feeling to the judgment of reason is, in most matters, a natural directional flow for right action. If, however, a wife feels that she is being bullied by *un*reason, it is entirely right for her to put her foot down and state, firmly, "My adherence is to the truth, not to your mere opinions."

⚡ Completing the Circle ⚡

There is a deeper truth in this supportive self-offering of the wife to the husband. The heart's energy, representing the feminine principle, needs to be directed upward to the center of will and spiritual vision in the forehead, which represents the masculine principle. Only thus can the heart's energy achieve its own fulfillment. When, instead, it flows outward to the world in the restlessness of likes and dislikes, the feelings become enmeshed in emotions, and, consequently, in delusion. The essence of yoga, or divine union, was expressed by the sage Patanjali in these words: *Yogas chitta vritti nirodh*—"Yoga is the neutralization of the vortices of the heart's feelings."

The consciousness can be truly centered in the spiritual eye only when it is joined there by love. Thence, the natural flow of spiritual development is outward, into the infinite. If, by contrast, reason flows downward in subservience to feeling, confusion results, and endless disharmony.

The masculine principle, when manifested to perfection, becomes absorbed in impersonal truth. The feminine principle, when brought to perfection, particularizes its absorption. That is to say, it seeks a focus through which to attain infinite consciousness. Thus, the masculine principle tends toward the abstract; the feminine, toward the particular. Either without the other would be incomplete.

In the end, these complementary aspects of human consciousness achieve perfection as though in the closing of a circle, at which point it is no longer possible to speak of either quality as having a beginning or an end. The circle is complete in itself.

◆》 Developing Impersonal Love 《◆

Marriage, to become a path to spiritual enlightenment, must be focused on the attainment, ultimately, of impersonal awareness. This, for many people, is not an easy concept to grasp, particularly as an ideal in the relationship between husband and wife. Yet it is not such an alien concept as may first appear. For true impersonality is not coldness or indifference to another's needs. Many monks and nuns, even, confuse impersonality with an aloofness that borders on pride. The only thing their detachment really shows, however, is their lack of sensitivity to others.

Impersonality, when rightly understood, is seen as the essence of kindness and selfless love. Impersonality means not to be selfishly attached to others, but to love them for *their* good rather than for one's own. It means thinking, not, "What can I *get out* of others?" but, "What can I *give to* them?"

The great danger in the married state lies in the thought, "He (or she) *owes* me something." This perception is both selfish and self-deluding. To depend on anyone else for the happiness we can find only within is to blind ourselves to the deepest truth of our own being. To make excessive demands of one's mate is to trample underfoot the tender petals of true love.

Perfect non-attachment comes only with long effort, to householders and renunciates alike. An important practice for achieving it is to seek occasional periods of silence and solitude. "Seclusion," Paramhansa Yogananda used to say, "is the price of greatness." In a spiritually focused marriage it is certainly possible, with mutual consent, to practice silence during certain periods of the day or week. Practice silence *together*. Recognize each other's need for occasional privacy. Find periods of time when you can be happily and lovingly silent together—not only in prayer and meditation, but while walking, or eating, or reading. Encourage each other to take a week or so every year for solitary prayer and meditation. Far from placing a strain on your relationship, such periods of seclusion will help to center your relationship more deeply in divine harmony and peace.

How often should you meditate together? That depends. In principle it is good, of course, to share your spiritual practices. Two people's rhythms, however, don't always coincide. Let your sharing be natural, never forced. One of you may prefer to meditate longer, or at different hours, than the other. If you give each other space in these matters, you will preserve a freshness in your relationship that would fade, were you to force them.

It is important to realize that your highest goal is not earthly perfection, but union with God. Strive to deepen your relationship together *in Him*. The closer you both come to God, the deeper will be the love you share between you. As Jesus Christ put it, "Seek ye first the kingdom of God, and His righteousness, and all these things shall be added unto you." (Matthew 6:33)

A final thought on the importance of silence: True love finds its highest expression in perfect stillness. Ultimately, it finds that expression in the breathless state of deep communion with the Infinite Beloved.

One way of developing impersonality in your love is to try always to behold in your partner, as if hidden by the veil of human personality, the Divine Presence. Work at becoming "other minded." See your partner as a manifestation of God's love, or as God's special gift to you—a gift meant not only for your comfort, but sometimes, also, for your spiritual training and discipline.

To help you in your efforts to rise above ego-conscious-ness, try not to accept anyone's self-definition—including your own spouse's—as an ego or personality. Accept, if you must, *the fact* that that is how others see themselves; respect their right to their own understanding. In your heart, how-ever, bow always to the Divine behind the mask. As you view others, including your own wife or husband, so they may come in time to view themselves.

❧ The Highest Duty ❧

An attitude of "other mindedness" is more difficult to maintain in marriage than in less intimate relationships. Ide-ally, your mate will be spiritually refined enough to appreciate and reciprocate in kind. Unfortunately, couples are not always so evenly matched, especially if the quest for God comes late in marriage, or to one partner alone. What are you to do, if your partner simply doesn't share your spiritual zeal?

Where understanding in these matters is not mutual, it is important never to attempt to "convert" your mate. Of-fer selfless love, instead. If a change is ever to come, it will be more likely to come as a result of your quiet example than of your admonishments, nagging or otherwise.

What about divorce? Is there a place for it in a spiritual marriage? Spiritual merit often lies in doing one's best under difficult circumstances; in this case, in living with someone who is not supportive of one's spiritual efforts. Nevertheless, the merit of sincere effort can also be overshadowed by the impossibility of success. In such cases, friendly separation may, sometimes, be a better solution than increasingly discouraging attempts at forging an unnatural bond together. There is no spiritual gain in a loving relationship that ends in bitterness.

For not every marriage is made in heaven, theological claims to the contrary notwithstanding. When a duty conflicts with a higher duty, it ceases to be a duty. Mankind's highest duty is to seek God, and truth. A marriage that gives this ideal a secondary place, in the name of a merely human compromise, is destined for failure on both levels, human and divine.

Life is always a compromise between our subjective expectations of it and its objective realities. Any compromise we make, however, should be adjusted to our principles, not our principles to the compromise.

Remember, tests are an inescapable part of the spiritual life—indeed, of life at every level. No problem is placed before us by our karma merely for our defeat. The greater the problem, the greater the potential for victory. *Yes*, it is more difficult, in some ways, to live a life of spiritual dedication within the home than living alone, or within the walls of a monastery. To accept, however, that marriage means *necessarily* to live for "me and mine," centered in the little ego rather than in the divine Self; or that the householder life is at best a path of spiritual compromise, is to accept patterns that can and must be changed.

☙ Living Examples of Spiritual Marriage ❧

What is needed more than anything else is role models of a new kind of marriage: expansive, not contractive; spiritual, not rooted in selfish desires. The epic of Rama and Sita is instructive and inspiring for all time, but *living* examples are needed also.

To this end, and to help provide a spiritual focus for many activities of modern life, I myself founded a community in 1968 called Ananda World Brotherhood Village. It is situated near Nevada City, California. There are, presently, five branch Ananda communities,* including one near Assisi, Italy. In these communities, single as well as married people live normal lives, but with a spiritual focus.

One reason I founded the Ananda communities was due to the realization that the same number of people, each one living and working in a different city, would not have nearly so great a social impact as if they concentrated their energies in one, or in a few, places. Ananda World Brotherhood Village today is famous throughout the world as a place that offers persuasive examples of new ways of living.

One of my hopes for these communities has been to evolve a new pattern for spiritual marriage. Despite many obstacles and difficulties in the attempt, a considerable and ever-growing number of marriages at Ananda are being looked to by people everywhere as sources of guidance and inspiration.

For information on Ananda and on how to visit it and observe at close hand our new solutions to the need for more relevant ways of living and interacting with others in modern times, please write to the publisher—or simply telephone Ananda's retreat facility, The Expanding Light, at 1-800-346-5350. The Expanding Light is open all year, and constantly hosts people from around the world.

This book is partly the outcome of experience gained at Ananda through twenty-six years of trial, error, and discovery. It is a book written, I might almost say, with blood, sweat, and tears—but also in triumph and in joy.

May the day dawn when people everywhere can embrace a new, ever more expansive consciousness in their lives, in the understanding that their own happiness must, necessarily, include the happiness of all.

* By 2012, their were eight branch Ananda communities in the U.S., Italy, and India.

Appendix

The following ceremony was written for couples who want their wedding to include the concept of expansive marriage. This ceremony has been performed many times.

A recording of the music is available from the publisher.

❧ Ananda Wedding ☙
Ceremony

Needed for the Ceremony:

- Candle for Puja Ceremony

- ROSES: 1 red, 1 white

- MATERIALS FOR CEREMONY OF THE ELEMENTS:
  Earth, Water, Incense

- MATERIALS FOR FIRE CEREMONY:
  Wood, Rice, Ghee

- Rings

- Rose Petals

- Marriage License

(Music was written for this ceremony, and is available from the publisher. Specific musical pieces are named below. Others may of course be substituted.)

❧ Ceremony ☙

Processional: *(Choir sings "Join Us in Blessing" while the marriage party enters in the following order: ministers, groom and best man, flower girls and ringbearers, bridesmaids, and bride with father.)*

Minister *(to audience):*

Please be seated.

Father's Offering: *(Father remains before altar holding the bride's hand through the following song.)*

Song: *("I Place My Daughter's Hand in Thine"—male solo)*

Minister *(leads the father):*

Father, I place this, my daughter's hand in Thine. Bless her and keep her, as, in Thy name, I have always sought to do.

Music

(Father returns to seat, as bride and groom kneel together at the altar, not yet holding hands. Minister(s) takes seat.)

Song: *("Blessed the Life"—choir)*

Song: *("Lord, May We Serve You"—choir)*

(The couple take their seats for the remainder of the music.)

Song: *("God, Our Father-Mother"—children)*

Instrumental: *("Galilee"—harp)*

Song: *("In the Spirit"—male solo)*

Song: *("When Human Hopes Toward Thee Aspire"—choir)*

Prayer: *(The minister, rising, asks the congregation to stand and leads them in prayer. After the prayer he asks them to sit down.)*

Talk: *(The Minister gives a short talk on the spiritual meaning of marriage.)*

Puja Ceremony

Minister:

Let us now join in jubilation as we lift up our hearts in song to the Lord. Please stand.

(First groom, then bride, then both together offer the lighted candle to the Masters, as the congregation joins in singing the following.)

Song: *("Father, Mother, Friend, Our God." Last two lines different than during The Festival of Light. All sing three times:)*

Father, Mother, Friend, our God,
We Thy wonders all acclaim.
May our thoughts be only of Thee;
Train our hearts to sing Thy name.

All desires born of delusion
Here we lay, Lord, at Thy feet.
In Thy Light we find our freedom.
In Thy love we drink Thy name.

Meditation

Minister: *(Asks everyone to be seated.)*

Let us all now meditate. Sit upright; close your eyes, and look upward. Concentrate your attention at the point between the eyebrows, and pray mentally, "Father, reveal Thyself." (pauses)

When you feel His inward touch, pray for God's grace on this couple as they seek divine blessing on their lives.

Chant: *("Ever New Joy, Gioia, Gioia, Gioia"—All sing.)*

Song: *("Woodland Devas"—duet, during meditation)*

Minister: *(Ends meditation by chanting AUM.)*

Exchange of Roses: *(The groom holds the red rose to be offered to the bride; the bride holds the white rose to be offered to the groom.)*

Minister *(to the couple):*

Take your roses, and offer them on the altar, placing them crosswise, the red rose over the white. The roses symbolize the love of your hearts, which you have dedicated first to God. The white rose symbolizes purity; the red, the ardor of faithful devotion. By placing them in the shape of a cross you signify your willingness to accept all trials with joy and faith in God; and your resolution always to give each other the strength to love Him more deeply. *(Give a short time for the couple to say a silent prayer at the altar.)*

Minister:

Now, retrieve your roses. Face each other.

(To the groom:) Take your rose in your right hand, and place it in her right hand, repeating after me: "Dear beloved, I offer you this rose as a symbol of my love for you, a love inspired by God, and offered to you as a channel of His love."

(To the bride:) Take your rose in your right hand, and place it in his right hand, repeating after me: "Dear beloved, I offer you this rose as a symbol of my love for you, a love inspired by God, and offered to you as a channel of His love.

(The couple sit.)

Song: *("Where He Dwells"—solo. If no soloist is available, the minister may read the words in blessing while the couple still kneel.)*

Where He dwells, the earth in gladness
Puts forth sweet herbs, shading trees.
Gay streams bound through summer meadows;
Fragrance blows on every breeze.
They with happiness are blessed,
Who the Lord have made their Guest.
Who the Lord have made their Guest.
Where He dwells, the earth in gladness
Puts forth sweet herbs, shading trees.

Ceremony of the Elements

Minister:

In all things see the hand of God;
And seek, through them, His blessing on your union.
From rocks and earth, seek steadfastness in love;
(He places a touch of earth on the forehead of each at the point between the eyebrows.)
From water and all liquid things:
the grace to flow through life in harmony,
without attachment,
in a spirit of acceptance and cooperation;
(He sprinkles water on their heads.)
From air and sweet fragrances:
pure freedom from all thought of "I" and "mine";
(He holds steadily between them a few sticks of smoldering incense.)
And from rising fire:
the understanding that human love
must ever aspire toward the heights
of perfect, divine love.
(He lights the sacrificial fire.)

Fire Ceremony

Minister:

In fire we see also a symbol
of the unifying power of God's love,
uniting your separate flames of life
in His one, infinite light.
Offer yourselves mentally into the fire of that love.

(To the couple:) Repeat after me.
O Infinite Love, I offer myself up to Thee.
Burn up and purify my limitations—
(Each offers a stick of wood into the flames.)
Destroy in me the seeds of earthly desire—
(They cast a handful of rice into the fire.)
Accept my pure aspiration to be one with Thee.
(They pour a little ghee into the flames.)

Holy Vows at Marriage

Minister:

Please kneel now before the altar, holding hands, and repeat after me:

Vows to God:

Beloved Lord,
We dedicate to Thee our lives, our service, and the love
we share.
May the communion we find with one another lead us to
inner communion with Thee.
May the service we render one another perfect in us our
service of Thee.
May we behold Thee always enshrined in one another's
forms.

May we always remember that it is above all Thee we love.

In every test of love, may we see Thy loving hand.
In any disagreement, may we seek Thy hidden guidance.
May our love not be confined by selfish needs,
>   but give us strength ever to expand our hearts
>   until we see all human beings, all creatures as our own.
Teach us to love all beings equally, in Thee.

(The couple now rise, and, standing, place their right hands together above the fire, while the minister covers their joined hands with his right hand. This next portion of the marriage vows they are to address to each other.)

Vows to Each Other:

Dear Beloved,
I will be true to you as I pray always to be true to God.
I will love you without condition, as I would be loved
>   by you—and as we are ever loved by God.
I will never compete with you; I will cooperate for our
own, and for all others', highest good.
I will forgive you always, and under all circumstances.
I will respect your right to see truth as you perceive it,
>   and to be guided as you feel deeply within yourself,
>   and I will work with you always, in freedom, to arrive
at a common understanding.

All that we do, may we do for God's glory.
May we live and grow together in His love and joy.

And may the offspring of our union—
>   whether human children or creative deeds—
>   be doorways for the inspiration that we feel from Him,
>   through each other.

May our love grow ever deeper, purer, more expansive,
  until, in our perfected love,
    we find the perfect love of God.

Visiting Priest's Blessing: *(If there is to be a blessing by a visiting priest, he should be invited up and asked to give it at this point.)*

Song: *("Thy Light Within Us Shining"—choir)*

Song: *("Divine Friendship."—If possible, sung by the couple, perhaps with help from one or two members of the choir.)*

Exchange of Rings

Minister:

Now, please take your rings.

(To the groom:) Repeat after me:

  "I, _____, take thee, _____, as my wife, to love,
  serve with in joyful harmony,
  and honor all the days of my life."

(To the bride:) Repeat after me:

  "I, _____, take thee, _____, as my husband, to love,
  serve with in joyful harmony,
  and honor all the days of my life."

Pronouncement

Minister:

In the name of God, Christ, and the great masters of
    our path,
I pronounce you married in the eyes of man and of God."

(The couple embrace and exchange a kiss.)

Blessing

Minister:

> May the blessings of God and the great ones be with you all the days of your lives.
>
> Go also with the blessings of all of us here assembled.

> *(He sprinkles them with rose petals, as symbols of divine blessing.)*

Recessional: (The recessional is to the accompaniment of instrumental music. The bride and groom, with the bride on the groom's right, lead the recessional. The attendants follow in pairs, with the minister last.)

About the Author

 Swami Kriyananda (J. Donald Walters) is one of the foremost proponents of yogic teachings in the world today. In 1948 at the age of twenty-two, he became a disciple of the Indian yoga master, Paramhansa Yogananda. He is one of a few remaining direct disciples of Yogananda active today. At Yogananda's request, Swami Kriyananda has devoted his life to lecturing and writing, helping others to experience the living presence of God within. He has taught on four continents in seven languages over the course of over 60 years. His teaching, audio and video recordings of his talks and music, and his many books translated into 28 languages have touched the lives of millions.

Swami Kriyananda has taken the ancient teachings of Raja Yoga and made them practical and immediately useful for people in every walk of life. His books and teachings on spiritualizing nearly every field of human endeavor include business life, leadership, education, the arts, community, and science. He has written extensive commentaries on the Bible and the Bhagavad Gita, both based on the teachings of Paramhansa Yogananda.

Swami Kriyananda is also known as the "father of the intentional communities movement," which began in the United States in the late 1960s. Inspired by Yogananda's dream of establishing spiritual communities, he founded in 1968 the first of what are now eight Ananda communities worldwide. They provide a supportive environment of "simple living and high thinking" where over 1,000 full-time residents live, work, and worship together.

The original 1946 unedited edition of Yogananda's spiritual masterpiece

Autobiography of a Yogi
Paramhansa Yogananda

Autobiography of a Yogi is one of the best-selling Eastern philosophy titles of all time, with millions of copies sold, named one of the best and most influential books of the twentieth century. This highly prized reprinting of the original 1946 edition is the only one available free from textual changes made after Yogananda's death. Yogananda was the first yoga master of India whose mission was to live and teach in the West.

In this updated edition are bonus materials, including a last chapter that Yogananda wrote in 1951, without posthumous changes. This new edition also includes the eulogy that Yogananda wrote for Gandhi, and a new foreword and afterword by Swami Kriyananda, one of Yogananda's close, direct disciples. Also available in unabridged audiobook (MP3) format, read by Swami Kriyananda, Yogananda's direct disciple.

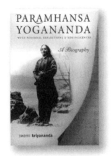

Paramhansa Yogananda
A Biography with Personal Reflections and Reminiscences
Swami Kriyananda

Paramhansa Yogananda's classic *Autobiography of a Yogi* is more about the saints Yogananda met than about himself—in spite of the fact that Yogananda was much greater than many he described. Now, one of Yogananda's few remaining direct disciples relates the untold story of this great spiritual master and world teacher: his teenage miracles, his challenges in coming to America, his national lecture campaigns, his struggles to fulfill his world-changing mission amid incomprehension and painful betrayals, and his ultimate triumphant achievement. Kriyananda's subtle grasp of his guru's inner nature reveals Yogananda's many-sided greatness. Includes many never-before-published anecdotes.

The New Path
My Life with Paramhansa Yogananda
Swami Kriyananda

This is the moving story of Kriyananda's years with Paramhansa Yogananda, India's emissary to the West and the first yoga master to spend the greater part of his life in America. With winning honesty, humor, and deep insight, Kriyananda shares his journey on the spiritual path through personal stories and experiences. Through more than four hundred stories of life with Yogananda, we tune in more deeply to this great master and to the teachings he brought to the West. This book is an ideal complement to *Autobiography of a Yogi*.

30-Day Essentials for Marriage
Jyotish Novak

The inspirational ideas in this full color gift book are fun, simple ways to enhance your marriage, helping you improve your life together in just thirty days—one thought for each day of the month.

Featuring one inspiring piece of advice and one practical exercise per day, this book is a useful, light-hearted, and eye-catching way for couples—whether engaged, newly married, or together for years—to quickly and gently deepen their relationship.

"Based on unusually deep understanding of the sacred mystical bond of marriage, it's a perfect gift for a partner, a newlywed couple, or sweethearts celebrating an anniversary." —East West Reviews

Education for Life
Preparing Children to Meet Today's Challenges
Swami Kriyananda

Kriyananda traces the educational crisis to an emphasis on technological competence at the expense of spiritual values, which alone can give higher meaning to life. Today the *Education for Life* system has been tested and proven for over three decades at the many Living Wisdom schools located throughout the world.

The Art of Supportive Leadership
A Practical Guide for People
in Positions of Responsibility
J. Donald Walters (Swami Kriyananda)

You can learn to be a more effective leader by viewing leadership in terms of shared accomplishments rather than personal advancement. Used in training seminars in the U.S., Europe, and India, this book gives practical advice for leaders and potential leaders to help increase effectiveness, creativity, and team building. Individual entrepreneurs, corporations such as Kellogg, military and police personnel, and non-profit organizations are using this approach.

Money Magnetism
How to Attract What You Need
When You Need It
J. Donald Walters (Swami Kriyananda)

This book can change your life by transforming how you think and feel about money. According to the author, anyone can attract wealth: "There need be no limits to the flow of your abundance." Through numerous true stories and examples, Swami Kriyananda vividly—sometimes humorously—shows you how and why the principles of money magnetism work, and how you can immediately start applying them to achieve greater success in your material and your spiritual life.

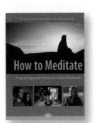

How to Meditate
A Step-by-Step Guide to the Art &
Science of Meditation
Jyotish Novak

This clear and concise guidebook has helped thousands since it was first published in 1989. With easy-to-follow instructions, meditation teacher Jyotish Novak demystifies meditation—presenting the essential techniques so that you can quickly grasp them. This newly revised edition includes scientific studies showing the benefits of meditation, plus all-new photographs and illustrations.

~ AUDIOBOOK AND MUSIC SELECTIONS ~

 Metaphysical Meditations
Swami Kriyananda

Kriyananda's soothing voice guides you in thirteen different meditations based on the soul-inspiring, mystical poetry of Paramhansa Yogananda. Each meditation is accompanied by beautiful classical music to help you quiet your thoughts and prepare for deep states of meditation.

 Meditations to Awaken Superconsciousness
Guided Meditations on the Light
Swami Kriyananda

Features two beautiful guided meditations as well as an introductory section to help prepare the listener for meditation. The soothing, transformative words, spoken over inspiring sitar background music, creates one of the most unique guided meditation products available.

 Relax: Meditations for Flute and Cello
Donald Walters
Featuring David Eby and Sharon Nani

This CD is specifically designed to slow respiration and heart rate, bringing listeners to their calm center. This recording features fifteen melodies for flute and cello, accompanied by harp, guitar, keyboard, and strings. Excellent for creating a calming atmosphere for work and home.

 AUM: Mantra of Eternity
Swami Kriyananda

This recording features nearly seventy minutes of continuous vocal chanting of AUM, the Sanskrit word meaning peace and oneness of spirit. AUM, the cosmic creative vibration, is extensively discussed by Yogananda in *Autobiography of a Yogi*. Chanted here by his disciple, Kriyananda, this recording is a stirring way to tune into this cosmic power.

How to Be Happy All the Time
The Wisdom of Yogananda Series, VOLUME 1

Yogananda powerfully explains virtually everything needed to lead a happier, more fulfilling life. Topics include: looking for happiness in the right places; choosing to be happy; tools and techniques for achieving happiness; sharing happiness with others; balancing success and happiness; and many more.

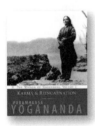

Karma & Reincarnation
The Wisdom of Yogananda Series, VOLUME 2

Yogananda reveals the truth behind karma, death, reincarnation, and the afterlife. With clarity and simplicity, he makes the mysterious understandable. Topics include: why we see a world of suffering and inequality; how to handle the challenges in our lives; what happens at death; and the purpose of reincarnation.

Spiritual Relationships
The Wisdom of Yogananda Series, VOLUME 3

This book contains practical guidance and fresh insight on relationships of all types. Topics include: how to cure bad habits that can end true friendship; how to choose the right partner; sex in marriage and how to conceive a spiritual child; problems that arise in marriage; the Universal Love behind all your relationships.

How to Be a Success
The Wisdom of Yogananda Series, VOLUME 4

This book includes the complete text of *The Attributes of Success*, the original booklet later published as *The Law of Success*. In addition, you will learn how to find your purpose in life, develop habits of success and eradicate habits of failure, develop your will power and magnetism, and thrive in the right job.

How to Have Courage, Calmness, & Confidence
The Wisdom of Yogananda Series, VOLUME 5

Winner of the 2011 International Book Award
~ Best Self-Help Title ~

This book shows you how to transform your life. Dislodge negative thoughts and depression. Uproot fear and thoughts of failure. Cure nervousness and systematically eliminate worry from your life. Overcome anger, sorrow, over-sensitivity, and a host of other troublesome emotional responses; and much more.

How to Achieve Glowing Health & Vitality
The Wisdom of Yogananda Series, VOLUME 6

Paramhansa Yogananda, a foremost spiritual teacher of modern times, offers practical, wide-ranging, and fascinating suggestions on how to have more energy and live a radiantly healthy life. The principles in this book promote physical health and all-round well-being, mental clarity, and ease and inspiration in your spiritual life. Readers will discover the priceless Energization Exercises for rejuvenating the body and mind, the fine art of conscious relaxation, and helpful diet tips for health and beauty.

Please visit our website to view our many other titles in books, music, audiobooks, e-books, spoken word, and DVDs:
www.crystalclarity.com

CRYSTAL CLARITY PUBLISHERS

Crystal Clarity Publishers offers additional resources to assist you in your spiritual journey including many other books, a wide variety of inspirational and relaxation music composed by Swami Kriyananda, and yoga and meditation videos. To see a complete listing of our products, contact us for a print catalog or see our website: www.crystalclarity.com

Crystal Clarity Publishers
14618 Tyler Foote Rd., Nevada City, CA 95959
TOLL FREE: 800.424.1055 or 530.478.7600 / FAX: 530.478.7610
EMAIL: clarity@crystalclarity.com

ANANDA WORLDWIDE

Ananda Sangha, a worldwide organization founded by Swami Kriyananda, offers spiritual support and resources based on the teachings of Paramhansa Yogananda. There are Ananda spiritual communities in Nevada City, Sacramento, and Palo Alto, California; Seattle, Washington; Portland, Oregon; as well as a retreat center and European community in Assisi, Italy, and communities near New Delhi and Pune, India. Ananda supports more than 75 meditation groups worldwide.

For more information about Ananda Sangha communities or meditation groups near you, please call 530.478.7560 or visit www.ananda.org

THE EXPANDING LIGHT

Ananda's guest retreat, The Expanding Light, offers a varied, year-round schedule of classes and workshops on yoga, meditation, and spiritual practice. You may also come for a relaxed personal renewal, participating in ongoing activities as much or as little as you wish. The beautiful serene mountain setting, supportive staff, and delicious vegetarian food provide an ideal environment for a truly meaningful, spiritual vacation.

*For more information, please call 800.346.5350
or visit www.expandinglight.org*